CHEKREPUBLIC

▌CHEK REPUBLIC

A REVOLUTION IN LOCAL TELEVISION ▌ DIANE DAKERS

VICTORIA · VANCOUVER · CALGARY

Heritage House Publishing Company Ltd.
heritagehouse.ca

LIBRARY AND ARCHIVES CANADA CATALOGUING IN PUBLICATION

Dakers, Diane M., author
     CHEK republic : a revolution in local television / Diane Dakers.

Includes index.
Issued in print and electronic formats.
ISBN 978-1-927527-99-3 (pbk.).—ISBN 978-1-77203-000-6 (html).
—ISBN 978-1-77203-001-3 (pdf)

     1. CHEK (Television station : Victoria, B.C.)—History. 2. Television broadcasting—
British Columbia—Vancouver Island. 3. Employee ownership. I. Title.

HE8700.9.C3D35 2014   384.5506'571128   C2014-903463-6   C2014-903464-4

Edited by Lara Kordic
Proofread by Lesley Cameron
Cover and book design by Jacqui Thomas
Cover and frontispiece photos courtesy of CHEK and TV image by subjug/iStockphoto.com

The interior of this book was produced on 100% post-consumer recycled paper, processed
chlorine free, and printed with vegetable-based inks.

Heritage House acknowledges the financial support for its publishing program from the
Government of Canada through the Canada Book Fund (CBF), Canada Council for the
Arts, and the province of British Columbia through the British Columbia Arts Council
and the Book Publishing Tax Credit.

 Canadian Patrimoine
Heritage canadien
 The Canada Council | Le Conseil des Arts
for the Arts | du Canada
BRITISH COLUMBIA
ARTS COUNCIL

18 17 16 15 14 1 2 3 4 5

Printed in Canada

Donald Mearns Dakers
1932 – 2013

This book is dedicated to my dad, who was
there at the beginning but never got
to see the finished product.

He was with me all the way.

FOREWORD

TELEVISION IS IN TRANSITION. The conventional model of appointment television is broken. Cable, satellite, specialty, pay TV, pay per view, the internet, Netflix, and social media are driving it toward its inevitable demise. How often have we heard this platitude? Yet over-the-air broadcasting still exists. And broadcasters are constantly searching for a new model that will allow it to survive.

To the north of the greatest and most productive entertainment industry in the world, Canadian television and its regulators have struggled from the outset to establish a system that reflects Canada and is not a pale copy of the US. This has always been a challenge given that the cost of production is the same whether a show is produced for the US or the Canadian market, but the market south of the border is ten times greater and thus offers greater economies of scale and greater returns (potentially tenfold greater).

Successive Canadian governments, following the advice of numerous commissions, passed progressive legislation, and with the aid of innovative regulators created a distinctive, flourishing, and diverse Canadian broadcasting system consisting of both public and private broadcasters. However, competitive pressures and the digital revolution have produced twin phenomena: the convergence of content and carriage, and the consolidation (both vertical and horizontal) of the Canadian communications industry.

No part of the industry suffered more from the impact of these phenomena than local television stations (and by corollary, local content). Nonetheless, Canadians' desire for local news and local content is as ardent as ever. In the context of political and economic globalization, there is something oddly reassuring about local news and content.

CHEK-TV, which emerged as a local independent broadcaster when Canwest Global Communications Corporation was taken over by Shaw Communications, builds its business case on this thirst for local news and content. Considered surplus to requirements by Canwest and slated for closure, CHEK was not given much of a chance to survive on its own. However, thanks to a dedicated staff, immense local support, and a fortuitous congruence of circumstances, CHEK is here today and hopefully will survive. The struggle was much harder than all the original players involved had anticipated.

CHEK Republic: A Revolution in Local Television tells that fascinating story. It lays out the historical broadcasting context and the structure of Canadian television—its challenges, the precarious role of independent stations, and the unanswered questions. Is there a way to viably sustain the production and dissemination of local news and content that Canadians desire? Are locally owned, over-the-air broadcasters like CHEK the answer? Are there lessons that can be drawn from CHEK's survival and applied elsewhere? No one knows the answers; only time will tell. In the meantime, readers will enjoy this passionate tale of CHEK's rebirth and survival.

Konrad von Finckenstein
Chair of the CRTC, 2007–12

one

A TWO-DOLLAR PLACE IN HISTORY

Some of the credibility and trust that's been lost in the media is because they're corporately owned. The corporate ownership model seems to be failing, so the future seems to be local ownership, independent ownership.

—**John Miller,** Ryerson University, 2009

ON SEPTEMBER 4, 2009, a two-dollar coin changed hands, sealing the deal for a mid-sized west coast television station. With that transfer of pocket change came a transfer of ownership that launched Victoria's CHEK as the first employee-owned television station in North America.

The transaction signalled the end of a whirlwind month of negotiations that had pitted Canada's largest media conglomerate against a few dozen Vancouver Islanders trying to save their workplace and their jobs.

Earlier that year, a financially flailing Canwest Global had tried to sell CHEK, along with a collection of other mid-sized television stations scattered across the country. In the end, the media giant managed to find buyers for some of those TV outlets—but not for CHEK. A few months later, Canwest announced it would simply pull the plug on the highly rated fifty-three-year-old Victoria broadcaster.

But the employees refused to let their workplace fade to black. They ponied up their retirement savings, rallied the community, pulled together investors, and lobbied politicians. They appealed to the Canadian Radio-television and Telecommunications Commission (CRTC), the governing body of broadcasting. And, amazingly, they pulled it off. The stars aligned that summer, and CHEK's employees bought themselves a TV station.

Immediately after the station changed hands, media observers dubbed the reinvented, employee-owned CHEK "an experiment in the future of local television," "a daring experiment," and "an example of the way the media landscape is being forever altered." Five years later, the two-fold CHEK experiment continues to test conventional wisdom about how TV should operate in this country. On the one hand is CHEK as an employee-owned entity—a small company struggling to survive in a highly corporatized, erratically regulated industry that does not favour independence. On the other hand is CHEK as a locally focused broadcaster—a community player flouting the accepted programming model for commercial TV, a model that insists that airing high-priced US shows is the way to go.

CHEK may be onto something here.

Six years ago, Leonard Asper, then-CEO of Canwest Global, declared the established model of Canadian commercial television to be "broken." And it's only become further fragmented since then.

The industry is changing, and changing so quickly that broadcasters can barely keep up. Audiences no longer look to traditional television as their prime source of broadcast news. Nor do they schedule their viewing time to watch their favourite shows. So-called appointment television barely exists these days. Viewers can now watch what they want to watch whenever, and wherever, they want to watch it. They watch the news online. They watch their must-see shows on iPads and cell phones. They PVR programs they like and fast-forward through commercials.

As viewing habits change, so do advertising patterns. Dollars once earmarked exclusively for TV ads are now divvied up among a variety of platforms as advertisers strive to reach new and different audiences. That means traditional media outlets are losing ground, and the race is on to find the secret to monetizing online and tablet content.

In this multimedia frenzy, CHEK remains focused on one thing—local news. "In the 500-channel universe, the one thing that still has value is local," said CHEK news anchor Jim Beatty. "In those 500 channels, who's going to tell you about . . . local firefighting efforts or the local car accident or the latest phone scam? Well, we are going to tell you that. You can't get that anywhere else. You can't get that on Netflix. You can't get that by going to the NASCAR channel or anywhere else. You get your local news here."

In addition to CHEK's focus on local content, the station's employee-ownership model is another experiment worth watching. It may be the only TV station in the nation operating under this ownership structure, but it's certainly not the only business doing it. Research shows that about 10 per cent of Canadian workers are involved in some form of employee-ownership model, and that model is on the rise in this country, in a variety of forms, across a wide range of businesses.

Calgary-based airline WestJet is probably the best-known example of an employee-owned organization in Canada—but buying in is not mandatory for staff. Employees who have opted into WestJet's stock option program collectively own 13 per cent of the company's shares.

Great Western Brewing Company's story is closer to that of CHEK. In 1989, new owner Molson announced it was shutting down the Saskatoon brewery (then called Carling O'Keefe). Instead of letting the sixty-two-year-old business fold, sixteen employees pooled their resources and bought it. The majority ownership of the brewery now lies with a small group of investors, but employees are still shareholders.

Similarly, when Harmac Pulp Mill in Nanaimo, BC, was slated for closure in 2008, 210 of its employees banded together with local investors to buy the business. Today, Harmac Pacific employs about three hundred people, each of whom has a financial stake in the company. When the CHEK employees decided to buy their TV station in 2009, they followed Harmac's example.

Five years in, though, the CHEK story is not the wild success observers had hoped it would be. What started as a David-purchases-from-Goliath tale has morphed into what Beatty calls "a little-engine-that-could story." The high of buying the station has been replaced by the reality of running it. Operating an independent TV station in this difficult economic and regulatory climate is a slog, plain and simple.

That's not to say the CHEK story isn't a tale of triumph. The employees achieved a remarkable feat when they defied all probability and bought the station. And the fact that the station is still on air five years later, despite the odds stacked against it, is a win for the workers and for the Victoria community. That said, CHEK remains an experiment-in-progress, constantly adapting its methods to accommodate changing conditions and unforeseen obstacles.

Still, the new CHEK model is a potential prototype still on the radar of industry insiders. In this era of rapid-fire technological change, as media outlets struggle to reinvent themselves, to remain relevant, and even to keep their doors open, the story of CHEK is worth watching.

That story is documented in this book.

MY INTEREST IN CHEK goes back to 1999, when I started working part-time for the station. I was there in the years just before and just after Canwest purchased CHEK. Since then, I have observed the station's rise and fall—and rise again—within the community.

In the summer of 2009, when Canwest announced it was shutting CHEK down, I wondered how that was even possible. How could a national media conglomerate simply pull the plug on a local TV station, no questions asked? Where was Canada's broadcast regulator in this process, and why did it permit corporate interest to take precedence over public interest? These were some of the questions I sought to answer in researching this book.

Like hundreds of other Vancouver Island residents that summer, I followed the CHEK story and supported the employees as they struggled to save their workplace. Because of my association with the Victoria media industry, and with CHEK specifically, I was privy to details that were never included in the public reporting of this story—the behind-the-scenes manoeuvring, political machinations, and apparent antagonism on the part of Canwest. All these elements added a level of complexity, and intrigue, to this story. But I wanted to know more.

Most of all, after the employees bought the station, I wanted to know whether CHEK's new approach to programming and operations could, in fact, be a potential prototype for other small and mid-sized TV stations in this country, as some pundits had predicted. Could the CHEK experiment herald a breakthrough for the future of television in this country?

This question became the focus of my grad thesis for my Master of Journalism degree at Carleton University in 2012. That grad thesis has evolved into this book—but it wasn't the simple evolution I expected it to be.

Just as I finished the thesis, the CHEK story took a surprising turn. The optimism among the employees early in the summer of 2012 turned to turmoil by summer's end. A serious blow to the bottom line threatened to sink the station. For almost two years, I wondered whether CHEK would survive as an employee-owned company. I delayed writing the final pages of this book many times, waiting for an ending—one way or another—to this chapter of the CHEK story.

In the spring of 2014, that ending finally came. Happily, though, it didn't mark the ending of CHEK. In fact, it was more of a new beginning. Today, CHEK remains a work-in-progress. The experiment continues.

two

SO MANY OUTLETS OWNED BY SO FEW

It remains the misfortune of most Canadian readers [and viewers] that they are served by fat, lazy, or one-sided media monopolies and that two royal commissions making modest recommendations to correct this were totally ignored.

—**Diane Francis,** *Controlling Interest: Who Owns Canada?*, 1986

IN 2009, TWO LOCAL television stations—CHEK in Victoria, BC, and CHCA in Red Deer, Alberta—were deemed expendable by their financially flailing owner. Canwest Global had tried to sell the stations. When it appeared no buyers could be found, the parent company opted to cut its losses and simply take the two stations off the air. In the end, only one of the stations (CHCA) faded to black. CHEK—thanks to the ingenuity of its employees, the vocal support of the Victoria-area citizenry, and the financial backing of a group of Vancouver Island investors—remains at Channel 6 on the dial today.

How did it come to this? How did Canadian television, which began as a collection of local, largely independently owned outlets get to the point where reflecting a station's community back to itself no longer had value? When did the business of the media become more important than the content of the media, the bottom line more valuable than the viewer?

How did Canadian government policies allow the industry to ultimately become what Carleton University's Dwayne Winseck once called "one of the most consolidated media systems in the developed world and an unrivalled scale of cross-media ownership," a system that sacrificed the local in favour of a centralized, regional and national, corporate structure.

TELEVISION IN CANADA DEVELOPED, in part, out of the Second World War. "One of the industries most vitally stimulated by the war was electronics, not the least part of which centred around the television industry," wrote E. Austin Weir in his 1965 book, *The Struggle for National Broadcasting in Canada.* With thousands of men returning from the battlefields, Canada needed a growth industry to employ them. At ᐧthe same time, Canadian television manufacturers were pushing for a national television service that would encourage Canadians to buy TV sets. The government of the day recognized that championing this new medium would solve two problems: it would create jobs while boosting manufacturers' bottom lines.

The government also recognized that any new television service must reflect Canadian culture, information, and educational programming to counterbalance the postwar influx of imported American programming. Taking all these elements into consideration, the government made what Weir called its "first pronouncement on television policy," in March 1949. The policy stated that the CBC board of governors was to be the governing body of the nation's television industry, and that the CBC was to set up production centres, immediately, in Toronto and Montreal, "to prepare the way for a national program service for itself and for private stations."

TV Trivia US public television broadcasting began in 1939, with commercial television following in 1941. Industry progress was slow during the Second World War, but picked up again in 1947–48.

In 1951, before a Canadian national television service existed, but because they could access American programming, Canadians owned 25,000 "television receiving sets," as the 1951 Massey Commission report called them.

Television 101: Tele-transcription Prior to the advent of videotape in the 1950s, the only means of recording a live television program for rebroadcast was to run a film camera in front of a TV monitor. The resulting film was called a kinescope. One particular network in the US, the DuMont Television Network, further developed this technology, calling it tele-transcription.

The ultimate goal was to have one private station in every Canadian city or region, and each private station would be required to broadcast a specified amount of CBC programming. Most importantly, "All network arrangements, whether by tele-transcriptions or physical links, were to be under CBC control."

Prime Minister Louis St. Laurent appointed the Royal Commission on National Development in the Arts, Letters and Sciences to study "the field of television, this new and unpredictable force in our society." Two years later, in 1951, this committee—better known as the Massey Commission in honour of its chair, Vincent Massey—supported the government's television policy. In its report, it recommended:

- That direction and control of television broadcasting in Canada continue to be vested in the Canadian Broadcasting Corporation.

- That no private television broadcasting stations be licensed until the Canadian Broadcasting Corporation has available national television programmes [sic] and that all private stations be required to serve as outlets for national programmes.

- That the Canadian Broadcasting Corporation exercise a strict control over all television stations in Canada in order to avoid excessive commercialism and to encourage Canadian content and the use of Canadian talent.

- That no private [television] broadcasting station operate in Canada as part of a network without the permission of the Canadian Broadcasting Corporation.

By the time the Massey Commission made these recommendations, the CBC had already hired staff, sending them to the US, Great Britain, and France to study the new medium. In September 1952, the national broadcaster launched Canada's first two television stations. Montreal's CBFT opened on September 6, and Toronto's CBLT went to air two days later.

The following January, the federal government, having reviewed the Massey Commission recommendations, made its second-ever policy announcement regarding the budding television industry. While again stressing the importance of Canadian content, it advocated for television to "spread as widely and quickly as possible to other areas," specifically Ottawa, Vancouver, Winnipeg, and Halifax, and it proposed to ask Parliament for money to build the necessary facilities. The government also said it was ready to take applications for private station licences to serve areas not covered by the CBC, but only one private station would be allowed in any given region.

With that, the federal government opened the door to independently owned TV stations and established a system of public-private ownership of the country's television industry. The CBC would own stations in six major centres, while exclusive television broadcast rights in other cities would be up for grabs by independent investors. All stations would create their own content, but would also carry the CBC's national programming—and all would be regulated by the CBC.

Within a year, Canada had its first two private television stations—Sudbury's CKSO and London's CFPL—marking the beginning of an "explosion" of stations across the country, wrote Weir:

> By December of 1954, there were nine stations and 1.2 million [TV] sets in Canada. Six months later, there were twenty-six stations and 1.4 million sets . . . By December of 1955, there were thirty-five stations in Canada; by December of 1957, forty-two. But the pace was slowing down, and the great explosion was over. By the end of 1959, there were thirty-eight private stations, and nine CBC stations (six English and three French).

During the television boom of the mid- to late 1950s, four private television stations opened in British Columbia, the first of which was Victoria's CHEK, on December 1, 1956. The others were CFJC in Kamloops (1957), CHBC in Kelowna (1957), and CJDC in Dawson Creek (1959). Vancouver's CBC station went to air in 1953. The first private station in Vancouver, CHAN, opened in 1960.

As private television stations flooded the Canadian market, so did criticism. Some detractors felt the requisite CBC programming was too "highbrow" and should cater more to the masses. Others didn't think taxpayers should have to financially support the national public broadcaster. "Above all, the role of the Corporation [the CBC] as both regulator of and competitor with the private stations was greatly resented," wrote W.H. Kesterton in his 1967 book, *A History of Journalism in Canada*. "Such issues became so acute that in 1955 the government appointed the Fowler Commission to investigate broadcasting and recommend measures for its improvement."

In 1957, this commission—officially known as the Royal Commission on Broadcasting, but commonly known by the name of its chairman, Robert Fowler—issued its report and recommendations. Most significantly, the Fowler Report proposed that television regulation be taken out of the CBC's hands and a new governing body be established to oversee public and private broadcasters. The government of the day, under Prime Minister John Diefenbaker, agreed, and in 1958 introduced a new Broadcasting Act that included the creation of the Board of Broadcast Governors (BBG). The task of this fifteen-member, government-appointed board was to "regulate the establishment and operation of networks of broadcasting stations, the activities of public and private broadcasting stations in Canada and the relationship between them." At the same time, the act created a second board, this one to manage the CBC. Oddly, this board reported directly to Parliament, bypassing the BBG and thwarting it in its mandate to oversee the public broadcaster.

The Fowler Report also recommended licensing new television stations *unaffiliated* with the CBC. This suggestion paved the way for the BBG to invite applications from private broadcasters to form a new network of so-called second stations in eight major markets—Halifax, Montreal, Ottawa, Toronto, Winnipeg, Calgary, Edmonton, and Vancouver. (The BBG did not have the authority to grant broadcast licences; it could only offer licensing recommendations.)

In 1961, after the federal government issued licences in these eight cities, and after much negotiation among the new stations' owners, the Canadian Television Network (CTN) was born, changing its name to CTV a year later. For the first time, the CBC faced competition.

Still, critics felt the system wasn't working. In 1964, the government once again called on Fowler to lead a study into "the ills of Canadian radio and television," as Kesterton put it. Specifically, this three-member committee was to look at the growing influence of American programming on Canadian audiences and to clarify ambiguities in the act relating to the roles of the BBG and the CBC.

In 1965, the Fowler Committee (not to be confused with the earlier Fowler Commission) made its report to Parliament. It criticized the performance of all parties involved in the broadcast industry—the BBG, the CBC, and private broadcasters—and said it was time the government established clear policies for the industry. It also suggested a new regulatory body, one that would be arm's-length from, but accountable to, government. The new broadcasting authority would replace the BBG and "would be responsible for the direction, supervision and control of the whole broadcasting system," wrote Kesterton.

Before the government adopted any of the Fowler Committee's suggestions, it initiated two more policy documents—a White Paper on Broadcasting (1966) and a report from the Standing Committee on Broadcasting, Film and Assistance to the Arts (1967). Both documents expressed concern over the potential for concentration and conglomeration of media ownership.

Parliament considered all three documents as it reworked its legislation. In the end, the new Broadcasting Act, adopted in 1968, incorporated the Fowler Committee's suggestion of doing away with the BBG, replacing it with the Canadian Radio Television Commission (CRTC).

Unlike the BBG, the new organization had the authority to issue broadcast licences. The CRTC's mandate also included establishing Canadian content requirements for broadcasters and ensuring that "the Canadian broadcasting system be effectively owned and controlled by Canadians."

The Broadcasting Act of 1968 remained in effect for the next twenty-three years, during which time issues of media concentration and cross-ownership became hot topics in the discussion, analysis, and regulation of Canada's media.

JUST AFTER THE NEW Broadcasting Act came into effect, Senator Keith Davey, a former radio station sales manager and self-professed "media groupie," suggested that the Senate strike a committee "to consider and report upon the ownership and control of the major means of mass public communication in Canada."

Released in December 1970, the resultant three-volume report—titled *The Uncertain Mirror: Report of the Special Senate Committee on Mass Media*—put the discussion about corporate ownership of the media in the spotlight for the first time. "The report provided Canadians with a comprehensive public examination of the media and . . . sounded alarm about the growing concentration of Canada's news industry," wrote *Toronto Star* public editor Kathy English in 2011.

Although the Davey Report, as it was commonly known, cited a few "pros"

TV Trivia Founded in 1968 as the Canadian Radio Television Commission, the CRTC changed its name to Canadian Radio-television and Telecommunications Commission in 1976—but retained the acronym.

with respect to concentrated media ownership—such as the ability of a large corporation to save a failing newspaper or broadcast outlet—it clearly saw the "cons" as more consequential. "The purpose of this Committee was not to ascertain whether concentration of media ownership is a Good Thing or a Bad Thing [*sic*]. Of course it is a bad thing," the report stated on its opening page. Two pages later, it continued:

> Control of the media is passing into fewer and fewer hands, and . . . the experts agree this trend is likely to continue and perhaps accelerate. The logical (but wholly improbable) outcome of this process is that one man or one corporation could own every media outlet in the country except the CBC. The Committee believes that at some point before this hypothetical extreme is reached, a line must be drawn . . . [A]t some point, enough becomes enough. If the trend towards ownership concentration is allowed to continue unabated, sooner or later it must reach the point where it collides with the public interest. The Committee believes it to be in the national interest to ensure that that point is not reached.

While the Davey Report insisted the government had no business in Canada's newsrooms when it came to content and editorial decisions, "the power to merge, the power to expand, the power to form large concentrations of media holdings, is another matter. We think the findings of this Committee demonstrate that concentration of ownership has proceeded to the point where some form of intervention by the state is desirable and necessary."

The report made a number of recommendations designed to curb the increasing corporatization and conglomeration of the nation's media outlets, suggestions that were largely ignored. Similarly ignored were the suggestions of another major study a decade later, the Royal Commission on Newspapers, better known as the Kent Commission.

Between the Davey Report and the Kent Commission, the 1978 Royal Commission on Corporate Concentration also commented on media concentration and cross-ownership. It recommended that "the

CRTC be empowered to prevent the owners of broadcasting stations from also owning newspapers and other print media that circulate in the same market."

The Kent Commission, led by former newspaper editor and civil servant Tom Kent, was born out of "Black Wednesday," the day Canada's two largest newspaper chains simultaneously shut down two major dailies in two major cities. On August 27, 1980, Southam Inc closed its *Winnipeg Tribune*, leaving Thomson Newspapers' *Winnipeg Free Press* as the only daily in the city; the same day, Thomson stopped the presses at the *Ottawa Journal*, leaving Southam's *Ottawa Citizen* as the only daily newspaper in the nation's capital. "Each closure gave the other chain a monopoly in that market, and it smacked of collusion," wrote Marc Edge in his 2007 book, *Asper Nation*.[1]

At the same time, Southam, which already owned the *Vancouver Province*, bought the *Vancouver Sun* from Thomson, giving Southam both daily newspapers in that city, while Thomson merged its recently acquired *Victoria Times* and *Daily Colonist*, forming the *Times Colonist*, the only daily in that city. Thomson also sold its stake in the *Montreal Gazette* to Southam—after closing the *Montreal Star* a year earlier—leaving Southam with a monopoly there as well.

Within a week of Black Wednesday, the Kent Commission had been established and charged with conducting an inquiry into the newspaper business in Canada. Less than a year later, on July 1, 1981, it tabled its report and proposed new legislation—a Canada Newspaper Act—that would, among other things, limit newspaper chains to owning a maximum of five daily newspapers, ban cross-ownership of newspaper and broadcast outlets in the same markets, and break up existing media monopolies:

> The Canada Newspaper Act must contain provisions to prevent any further increase in concentration and to reduce the worst features of the concentration that has hitherto been allowed. While the local monopoly of a newspaper is a problem in itself . . . the worst feature of concentration is not the ownership of several newspapers by one company; it is their ownership by a "conglomerate," a company having, or associated with, extensive other interests.

While some of the Kent Commission's recommendations were drafted into legislation under the Liberal government of Prime Minister Pierre Trudeau, most never made it into law. The one exception was a 1982 directive to the CRTC to deny broadcast licences to media organizations that already owned daily newspapers in the same market they were applying to broadcast into. The directive—officially called PCO 2294, where PCO stands for Privy Council Office—was designed to make explicit something the CRTC had already been doing implicitly. "The directive reinforced their policy and gave it a legal sanction which it previously didn't have," said Alan Darling, one of the lawyers charged with drafting PCO 2294.[2]

The directive also allowed for exceptions "when such a rule would cause unfair hardship or when the market is extremely competitive." Over the next three years, until Prime Minister Brian Mulroney's government rescinded the directive, "this exception was applied to nearly every case heard by the Commission," wrote Joseph Jackson in 1999 in *Newspaper Ownership in Canada*.

Between 1985, when PCO 2294 died, and 1991, when the twenty-three-year-old Broadcasting Act was revamped, "the policy debate droned on," wrote McGill University's Marc Raboy.

First came the Caplan-Sauvageau Task Force on Broadcasting Policy (1986), which recommended the government take a stand on media concentration. In 1988, the CRTC held public hearings, and Flora MacDonald, then Minister of Communications, published her own broadcast policy statement and introduced Bill C-136. That, in turn, generated ninety-two amendments and nine days of debate before Prime Minister Mulroney mooted the whole process by requesting the Governor General dissolve Parliament and call an election.

During this time, continued Raboy,

The Canadian broadcasting system continued to evolve without any of the necessary new checks required by the new context. The CRTC completely rewrote its radio, television and cable regulations, and declared it would henceforth take a "supervisory" approach to its task, relying on industry to adopt measures of "self-regulation." . . . In the private sector, the concentration of ownership among a shrinking handful of giant corporations rose to a new height, in the name of the need to be competitive on a global scale. New "specialty" television services were licensed for cable distribution, amid waves of controversy surrounding the proposed funding and programming formulas. All the while, the Americanization of Canadian broadcasting continued apace.

Once the Mulroney government was reinstalled in November 1988, it quickly retabled Bill C-136—now called Bill C-40—which finally, after *another* sixteen months of debate, became the new Broadcasting Act on February 1, 1991.

One more legislative change is worth mentioning here—the replacement of the Combines Investigation Act with the Competition Act in 1986. Under the former, mergers and monopolies were illegal and subject to criminal proceedings, as newspaper giants Thomson and Southam experienced in 1981. Having said that, of the nine media cases brought before the courts during the act's seventy-five-year history, seven resulted in acquittals, and the other two defendants pleaded guilty. "Media mergers before 1986 had what was, in practice if not in theory, a free ride," stated the 2006 *Final Report on the Canadian News Media*. Under the new Competition Act, such mergers have become civil matters, with a lighter burden of proof—and the only "competition" in question is the competition for advertising dollars.

AS THIS DECADE OF policy comings and goings progressed, so did Israel ("Izzy") Asper's Canwest Global. What had begun in 1975 in Winnipeg as a single-station television company was, by 1990, a collection of five stations in four provinces—BC, Saskatchewan, Manitoba, and Ontario—and it had already started to raise the ire of its competitors.

During a 1990 CRTC transfer-of-ownership hearing to approve Asper's buyout of his business partners, Canwest's competitors (specifically CTV) argued that, under Asper's full control, Canwest Global would be a "network," and should, therefore, be subject to the same rules as Canada's other conventional networks, the CBC and CTV. The

CRTC disagreed, satisfied that each of Canwest's stations was independent enough that the company's operations did not fit the definition of a network as defined by the Broadcasting Act.[3] Instead, the CRTC dubbed Canwest Global a "system," meaning (among other things) it wouldn't be held to the same standards

Television 101: Simultaneous Substitution

Designed to help Canadian broadcasters offset the cost of importing American programming, the simultaneous substitution rule states that if a US program airs in Canada on an American station—via cable or satellite—at the same time it airs on a Canadian station, the Canadian company can sell local advertising to run on both stations at the same time, effectively doubling that station's revenue.

as its competitors were when it came to producing Canadian content.

Because Canwest was permitted to spend fewer dollars creating new programs, it had more money to spend on importing American shows. At the time, the cost of importing an American drama series was about 10 per cent of the cost of a similar locally produced show. Not only did this give Canwest a financial leg-up over CBC and CTV, it also positioned Asper's company to take full advantage of the CRTC's "simultaneous substitution" rule, further boosting the company's bottom line.

"This degree of carefully constructed and fiercely defended regulatory freedom has allowed CGS [the Canwest Global System] to become the most profitable television broadcasting entity in Canada," wrote Paul Taylor in a 1993 issue of the *Canadian Journal of Communication*.

Over the next few years, as Canwest applied for licence renewals for its various stations, the CRTC started to voice concerns about the broadcaster's lack of local production, its practice of airing its limited Canadian content during non–prime time hours and its failure to meet its licensing conditions in general. In 1992, for example, the CRTC renewed Global's Ontario licence for four years, rather than the standard seven, stating that "while Global has generally met the requirements of its conditions of licence, it may not have contributed to the Canadian broadcasting system as fully as it should have, given the resources available to it."

On the same day the CRTC renewed Global's Ontario licence, it also issued a public notice titled *New Flexibility with Regard to Canadian*

Program Expenditures by Canadian Television Stations. This document allowed broadcasters to miss their spending targets, in terms of local-content creation, by as much as 5 per cent in any given year, as long they met their financial obligations over the term of their licence renewal periods. In 1995, the CRTC again modified the Canadian content rule, this time giving broadcasters the freedom to choose whether they would meet their local production commitments quantitatively (via a set dollar value) or qualitatively (through a set number of hours of programming), opening the door for broadcasters to fill their quota with cheaply produced, second-rate programming.

It was policy changes like these—flexibilities that favoured "market logic and industry profitability rather than the public interest"—that led Concordia University's Neil Barratt to suggest in 2008 that the CRTC was guilty of "regulatory impotence," "industry bias," and taking "a hands-off approach" in its role as broadcast industry watchdog:

> Regulation in Canadian broadcasting . . . more often takes the shape of a business consultant than an advocate of the public interest. Repeatedly . . . requests for leniency, reductions, and flexibility, as well as outright failure to meet commitments, have been met with explicit approval of the broadcast industry's sole regulatory body.

But Canwest Global wasn't the only media corporation to benefit from what Carleton University's Dwayne Winseck called the CRTC's "shift from *preventing* to *promoting* convergence."

WHILE THE DOOR TO horizontal media convergence was thrown wide open by the Mulroney government in 1985 when it repealed PCO 2294, the gateway to vertical convergence was unlocked more gradually.

It started in 1993, with the "quiet elimination" of the federal Department of Communications (DoC), a ministry that had been created twenty-four years earlier. "Its raison d'être was to bring communication technologies together with their content within the same framework," wrote media scholars Bram Dov Abramson and Marc Raboy in 1999.

The DoC oversaw the CRTC and had jurisdiction over content and carriage, a single body that "juxtaposed medium with message."

When the Mulroney government abolished the DoC, it divvied up the department's responsibilities. The newly created Department of Canadian Heritage was to oversee the CRTC

Television 101: Convergence Horizontal convergence occurs when one company acquires related businesses within the same industry—for example, a newspaper owner acquires a television station. Vertical convergence occurs when a company in a given industry acquires a business that operates in another stage of the same industry—for example, a television network acquires a television production company.

and the cultural, or Canadian content, aspects of broadcasting, while Industry Canada would take charge of telecommunications policy and infrastructure issues. In short, the move split responsibility for medium and message. "Dispersal of the DoC meant . . . the separation of policy-making for content and carriage in the moment of their convergence," wrote Abramson and Raboy.

This division of responsibility necessitated the creation of new communication policies. Between 1994 and 1996, the CRTC and the government (now a Liberal government under Prime Minister Jean Chrétien) issued reports, held public hearings, made policy proposals, and discussed communications policy at length. In the end, Canadians were left with a system that merged what one report called "the two solitudes of the Canadian communications system"—broadcasting and telecommunications. That meant telecommunications and cable companies were now free to own television stations, and vice versa. And that, said Marc Edge, ultimately opened the door for a "wave of multimedia deal-making" a few years later. In a 2011 article in *Media, Culture & Society*, he summarized:

Convergence transformed Canada's media landscape in 2000 to a much greater extent than in the U.S. or other countries with restrictions on cross-ownership . . . By the end of that year, Canada's two private television networks had partnered with national newspaper properties, as had the largest privately owned French-language network in the province of Quebec. CTV, the country's largest private network, was acquired by telecom giant Bell Canada Enterprises, which then partnered with the *Globe and Mail* national newspaper to create a Cdn $4 billion multimedia enterprise initially known as Bell Globemedia. Canwest Global Communications, which owned the national network Global Television, bought Canada's largest newspaper chain, Southam Inc, for Cdn $3.2 billion. Quebecor, a newspaper company that started in Quebec but had expanded nationwide with its 1998 purchase of the Sun Media newspaper chain, then paid Cdn $5.4 billion for Quebec's largest cable company, Groupe Videotron, which owned the TVA network in Quebec.

For McGill University's Darin Barney, the CRTC's approval of these mergers "clearly signaled the priority of current Canadian policy to permit unprecedented levels of consolidation, concentration and cross-ownership in communication industries." Carleton University's Dwayne Winseck agreed. "In an amazingly short period of time, cross-media ownership [went] from being the exception to the norm."

This turn-of-the-century wave of media convergence was cause enough for concern that the Standing Committee on Canadian Heritage conducted an "urgent review" of Canada's broadcast system "to determine whether the ideals and objectives set out in the Broadcasting Act of 1991 were being met and whether the Act itself was in need of reform." One of the six themes the Standing Committee set out to address in its research was ownership—including "patterns of ownership, cross-media ownership and vertical integration."

In its 2003 report, *Our Cultural Sovereignty: The Second Century of Canadian Broadcasting*, the committee acknowledged the difficult position it found itself in with respect to ownership concerns:

In Canada, cross-media ownership has reached unprecedented heights with the media takeovers that occurred in 2000. The problem the Committee has confronted is how to address this situation, given that it is faced with the *fait accompli* of convergence, consolidation and concentration. This means making recommendations that will ensure that citizens can have access to a variety of viewpoints, without throwing the Canadian media industry into financial turmoil. This is perhaps the most delicate issue that the Committee has had to address.

The report went on to outline a number of options, ranging from "take no action and let the issue be resolved by the marketplace" to "the outright prohibition of cross-media ownership." In the end, it recommended—as had many reports in the past—that the government "issue a clear and unequivocal policy" on cross-media ownership. In addition, it suggested that the CRTC neither award nor renew broadcast licences involving cross-media ownership until such a policy was in place.

Just before the Standing Committee on Heritage issued its findings, the Standing Senate Committee on Transportation and Communications began its own examination of "the current state of Canadian media industries." In April 2004, it released an *Interim Report on the Canadian News Media*, summarizing the findings of the committee to date.

In discussing media concentration, one unidentified committee member stated: "I do not think anything has consumed our time more in our discussions with our various witnesses than cross-ownership." Without apparent judgment, the interim report summarized the situation:

> The media consolidation of recent years has been a worldwide phenomenon of massive proportion. Most notable was the transaction in the U.S. in 2000 involving AOL and Time-Warner, a transaction valued at billions of dollars and bringing together content, carriers and new media. The transaction became the symbol for convergence, and media firms around the world followed. In Canada, BCE [Bell Canada], Canwest Global and Quebecor acquired other media companies—and considerable debt in the process—and became media giants with significant cross-media ownership.

Two years later, in its *Final Report on the Canadian News Media*, the Senate Committee *did* pass judgment—on the CRTC and the Competition Bureau for their regulatory impotence. "It is reasonable to ask: Why did our laws or regulators fail to prevent the extent of concentration that we see in these [Canadian] markets today?"

The report reiterated the 1970 Davey Report assertion "that the government has no role in the newsrooms of the nation," but "the media's right to be free from government interference does not extend . . . to a conclusion that proprietors should be allowed to own an excessive proportion of media holdings in a particular market, let alone the national market. Yet the current regulatory regime in Canada does little to prevent such an outcome."

. Like the Davey Report, the Kent Commission, and the Heritage Committee report (2003), this report called on the government to establish clear policies to regulate concentration of media ownership, noting that Canada is "atypical among large democracies" in its lack of such policies. France, the UK, Australia, Germany, and the US all had policies restricting media concentration and cross-ownership. The problem in Canada, said the *Final Report*, is that administration of media legislation is divided between agencies with divergent agendas—the CRTC, which is governed by the Broadcastings Act, and the Competition Bureau, which falls under the Competition Act.

The Competition Act is "an economic law" that "covers all businesses in Canada . . . [and] has no specific provisions regarding broadcasting, telecommunications, newspapers or other media." It does not take into account such things as cross-media ownership and diversity of voices within individual communities or across the country. On the other hand is the CRTC, which "has largely set aside its concerns about news and information. Instead, the CRTC focuses on 'cultural' issues, i.e., policing Canadian content." Neither act considers "public interest" in its decisions regarding media mergers, meaning "the current regulatory system offers little protection against particular adverse effects of ownership concentration on the diversity of voices."

The *Final Report on the Canadian News Media* concluded that the government should establish a system requiring the CRTC and the Competition Bureau to work together when it comes to media mergers.

The process should "include clear accountability for the consideration of the public interest. This is in sharp contrast to the current situation where no regulatory organization is ultimately accountable." In addition, the CRTC should be mandated to hold public hearings to consider the impacts on public interest when ruling on mergers that include broadcasting organizations.

The most effective way to proceed would be to enact a new section of the *Competition Act* to deal with the mergers of news gathering organizations. This new section should include the following assessment criteria:

- Cross-media ownership in particular markets;
- Development of a dominant position in particular advertising, production or distribution markets;
- Mergers that involve acquiring more than, say, 35 per cent of a particular audience, or subscribers.

As of today, none of the recommendations suggested in the final report of the Standing Committee on Canadian Heritage or the subsequent *Final Report on the Canadian News Media* have been adopted.

DESPITE THE REPORTS AND recommendations of the early 2000s, media convergence continued, unhindered—some would say even supported—by government regulation.

"The government recognizes that convergence has become an essential business strategy for media organizations to stay competitive in a highly competitive and diverse marketplace," wrote Bev Oda, then Minister of Canadian Heritage and Status of Women, in her official response to the *Final Report on the Canadian News Media*. She added that "the current legislative, regulatory, and policy frameworks, supported by various government programs, has served Canadians well"—thus rejecting any change in policy.

Since the *Final Report on the Canadian News Media* was released, though, media consolidation has increased. "In 2006," wrote Marc Edge,

"CTVglobemedia paid $1.4 billion[4] for several dozen radio and television stations owned by Toronto-based CHUM Ltd. [In 2007], Canwest flouted foreign ownership limits by partnering with New York investment bank Goldman Sachs in scooping up a baker's dozen cable television channels from Alliance Atlantis."

After this pair of landscape-changing takeovers, the CRTC announced it would hold yet another public hearing, this time "to review its approach to ownership consolidation and other issues related to the diversity of voices in Canada." On January 15, 2008, it released its resultant *Regulatory Policy: Diversity of Voices*, which contained two noteworthy, but ultimately ineffectual, directives. The first prohibited a single company from owning television, radio, and newspaper outlets in a given market. (The *National Post* and *Globe and Mail*, as national newspapers, were exempt from this rule.) In a next-day news story about the release of the new CRTC policy, *Globe and Mail* reporter Grant Robertson wrote:

> That change was considered inconsequential by critics of media consolidation who said it will have little effect since Canwest doesn't own radio assets across Canada and CTVglobemedia isn't invested in local papers. "There are no cases in Canada where somebody owns all three," said Lise Lareau, president of the Canadian Media Guild. "It doesn't change anything."

The new policy also stated that no one company would be permitted to control more than 45 per cent of the over-the-air television market, and the CRTC would "carefully examine" transactions that would give a single owner between 35 and 45 per cent. This rule, predicted Robertson, "will have the bigger impact and may slow a trend of recent media consolidation driven by a rush to acquire specialty channels. CTVglobemedia (owner of CTV, TSN, MTV and others) already has 37.4 per cent of the English TV audience. Canwest (owner of Global, Showcase, HGTV and others) has 26.3 per cent."

Four years later, in October 2012, the CRTC appeared to make good on its promise to limit control of the airwaves when it rejected

Bell Canada's proposed $3.4 billion takeover of Astral Media, citing concerns over "an unprecedented level of consolidation in the Canadian marketplace."

Eight months later, though, after Bell submitted a revamped proposal, the CRTC approved the merger—with some modifications. The original proposal would have given Bell a 35 per cent share of French and 45 per cent share of English television viewership. The modified deal left the corporation with 23 per cent of the French market and 36 per cent of the English market.

Until the CRTC sanctioned the Bell-Astral merger in 2013, the trend toward media consolidation had, in fact, slowed down, but not because of any policy decisions. As it turned out, the more prominent factor in slowing the pace of media consolidation was the global economy. An early-twenty-first-century recession, which hit a few years after the convergence whirlwind of 2000, hobbled some of Canada's major media corporations. But a more serious economic downturn beginning in 2008 led to many of these same companies being "restructured . . . dismantled . . . collapsed in financial ruin . . . or [abandoning] early visions of convergence altogether," said Carleton University's Dwayne Winseck.

A number of these organizations, most notably Canwest Global, had taken on massive debt loads to finance their expanding empires and could no longer pay their creditors. Throughout the first decade of the twenty-first century, Canwest consolidated its newsrooms, sold international assets, and closed news bureaus in its efforts to keep creditors at bay. In the summer of 2009, Canwest sold two of its secondary television stations in Canada and decided to simply shut down two others—Victoria's CHEK and Red Deer's CHCA. This move to eliminate all but its metropolitan Global stations signalled that Canwest was prepared to sacrifice the local in an attempt to preserve the corporate. In doing so, it validated a concern cited by the Standing Committee on Canadian Heritage in its 2003 final report:

> The Committee is concerned that community, local and regional broadcasting services have become endangered species, and that many parts of Canada are being underserved. In its travels across the country, the Committee heard from

a surprising number of citizens who felt that they had been neglected and even abandoned by the broadcasting system.

Ultimately, citizens in Victoria, BC, refused to be abandoned by the broadcasting system. If Canwest didn't want to keep CHEK on the air, they insisted the company should sell the station to a group of people who did.

three

THE ASPER EMPIRE

Media empires are not permanent and omnipotent but rather are subject to the internal needs of organizations and bureaucracies, as well as external economic, financial, and regulatory forces.

—Media economist **Robert Picard**, *The Tyee*, 2008

The Rise and Fall of Canwest Global

In the first few years of the twenty-first century, Canwest Global was the largest mainstream media conglomerate in Canada. At its height, the company owned 17 television stations across the country, 21 specialty television stations, the *National Post*, 13 daily newspapers, 126 community newspapers, a radio station, and a number of websites.

"In its heyday, the Canwest media empire employed more than 10,000 spread over four continents, and reached 30 million viewers and readers daily," wrote Peter C. Newman in *Maclean's* in April 2009. "Its Canadian TV channels were the country's most profitable, with 16 per cent of the national viewing audience, and 30 per cent of the profits."

Then it all came crashing down.

CANWEST'S HISTORY DATES BACK to the early 1970s, when Israel Harold ("Izzy") Asper, a tax lawyer and Manitoba Liberal MLA, responded to the Canadian government's 1973 call for applications for independent television licences. Asper partnered with his executive assistant, Peter Liba, and a pair of investors, Paul Morton and Seymour Epstein, to submit a bid for the Winnipeg licence. The group entered its application in Morton's name to avoid a potential "political stink for Liberal Ottawa to be seen handing the station to one of the party's provincial leaders," wrote Edward Greenspon in *Report on Business Magazine* in 1988. Western Manitoba Broadcasters Ltd., later known as Craig Media, also applied for the Winnipeg licence but lost to Asper's group.

Rather than build a station from the ground up, Asper and his partners set their sights on taking over KCND, a small TV outlet based in Pembina, North Dakota, about a hundred kilometres south of the Manitoba capital. Even though KCND was an American station, it competed for Winnipeg viewers, and the bulk of its advertisers were Winnipeg-based.

Armed with their new broadcast licence, Asper and company let it be known they could set up a new transmitter between Pembina and Winnipeg, effectively blocking the KCND signal from its northern viewers. Rather than risk losing his audience—and his advertising dollars—KCND's owner agreed to sell to Asper's group.

"Over the 1975 Labour Day long weekend, Canwest hired a fleet of trucks and shipped the station across the border," wrote Marc Edge in his 2007 book, *Asper Nation*. "It was reassembled inside a vacant Winnipeg supermarket, and Canwest reversed the first two letters of the station's call sign to conform to CRTC protocol."

CKND-TV, Canwest's first television station, took to the airwaves on September 1, 1975, with a program of opening ceremonies followed by the Jerry Lewis Telethon from Los Angeles.

Meanwhile, the Global Television Network had also begun broadcasting. With a central studio in suburban Toronto—and six transmitters spreading the signal across southern Ontario, from Windsor to Ottawa—the regional broadcasting operation had gone to air on January 6, 1974. One of Global's founders was broadcaster Al Bruner, who later offered Asper some advice on setting up a TV station. The two men also discussed sharing programming on their upstart stations.

"Al Bruner and I schemed and dreamed," said Asper in a *Playback* magazine article in 1999. "We were the pioneers of what we called the third force. It was such an outrageous idea at the time—that these little fledgling stations would one day be an equivalent to CTV. We believed that with Global as the flagship, there would emerge a strong programming relationship between all the new independent stations."

Within a few months of its launch, though, Global was virtually bankrupt and needed a financial bailout. Seymour Epstein, one of Asper's partners and an investor in Global, "realized that the station's problem wasn't a design failure so much as a matter of pilot error," wrote Greenspon in *Report on Business*. He knew it could be a success, so he recruited Asper, Morton, and "a crackerjack radio operator named Allan Slaight" to save the insolvent enterprise. Together, the quartet snapped up the fledgling network for $11.2 million in April 1974.

Three years later, the quartet became a trio when Slaight made his exit. By then, the Global Television Network was thriving, but the relationship among its principals had deteriorated dramatically. When Slaight took a $6.8 million buyout early in 1977, he left Global in the hands of Canwest (Asper's company, with partner Gerald Schwartz) and Odeon Morton Theatres Ltd. (Morton and Epstein's company) in a 50–50 ownership arrangement.

That same year, 1977, Canwest took its first steps into international broadcasting with a San Francisco–based pay TV operation called Universal Subscription Television (USTV). Five years later, Canwest sold USTV "over Asper's objections," wrote Marc Edge, to help offset the recession-induced financial losses of some of Canwest's non-broadcast entities.

At this point, disagreements over company operations led Asper and Schwartz to go their separate ways. In 1983, they split Canwest, with Asper retaining the thriving television properties and Schwartz taking the rest, laying the foundation for what would become his Onex Corporation.

Throughout the late 1970s and through the 1980s, combined profits of Canwest and Global soared, thanks in part to a CRTC subtlety. At this point, the two companies remained separate entities and, because the CRTC considered their joint collection of stations a television "system" rather than a "network," it wasn't subject to the same restrictions as were CBC and CTV, which were national networks.

"The Canadian content requirements set down by the CRTC for third television stations [non-network stations] were not as strict as the 60 per cent required of the CBC and CTV networks," wrote Edge. "By the time CKND's licence came up for renewal in 1977, however, local content made up only 20 per cent of its programming, compared to the 50 per cent it had promised" when it got the original licence.

That meant the Canwest-Global system was airing inexpensive US programs rather than creating costly local productions. That translated into increased dollars for the company's coffers to support its rapid growth. "The mounting profits were used to add more Canadian stations, expand overseas and ultimately acquire Southam [newspapers]," wrote Edge.

In 1987, Canwest built a pair of Saskatchewan stations—CFRE in Regina and CFSK in Saskatoon. Two years later, it took full ownership of Vancouver's CKVU, an independent outlet in which it had first invested a decade earlier.

At the same time, strife within the upper echelons of Global TV was once again shaking the company's core. This time, Asper found himself in a court battle with Morton and Epstein, and in 1989, after a five-year fight for control of the company, a Manitoba judge ordered an end to the long-time partnership. The two sides were forced into an auction for control of Global, an auction Asper's Canwest Communications ultimately won with a bid of $131 million. Canwest, with Asper at the helm, was now in full control of the Global Television Network.

Throughout the 1990s, Asper's business, now called Canwest Global Communications, was at the top of its game. It "handily dominated the ratings," wrote Grant Robertson and Andrew Willis in a 2009 *Globe and Mail* article, "with shows such as *Seinfeld* and *Friends* pulling in advertising dollars by the tens of millions in a good week."

At the same time, the company started a serious push to acquire international media properties. "[Asper] was not content for Canwest to be a wildly profitable player, secure in its Canadian niche," wrote Steve Maich in *Maclean's* in October 2009. "The empire was called Canwest Global, and he was determined to make the second part mean something." Maich suggested this may have been Asper's first mistake:

His primary achievement was to amass a collection of regional television stations in an era when broadcast permits were government-issued licenses [*sic*] to print money. He filled his airtime mainly with American network programs, onto which he would graft Canadian ads. That was smart business and it made him phenomenally rich—but let's not confuse this with visionary entrepreneurship. In fact, the problems really began when Izzy started dreaming big.

In 1991, New Zealand's cash-strapped TV3 needed investors. When the government eased up on its foreign ownership rules, Canwest bought 20 per cent of the station, gradually building up to 100 per cent ownership in 1997. The following year, Canwest helped rescue Australia's faltering Network TEN with an infusion of about $130 million, buying itself a controlling stake in the company Down Under. In the mid-1990s, Canwest also bought—and subsequently sold—interests in Chilean television and British radio stations.

In 1997, Canwest launched a second New Zealand television station and bought a network of seven radio stations. Over the next five years, it built up this network to the point where Canwest owned almost half of all radio in New Zealand.

In 1998, Canwest moved into Ireland, leading a group of investors in launching the country's first private television network—also called TV3. "Within two years, Canwest had acquired 90 per cent of TV3 [Ireland], but in late-2000, it sold half . . . for $62.2 million," wrote Edge in *Asper Nation*. "The deal provided Canwest with needed capital to complete its [2000] purchase of Southam from Conrad Black."

WHILE CANWEST WAS HITTING the airwaves internationally, it was also making waves at home.

In 1994, Asper took a step toward his dream of owning a Canada-wide television system when he purchased (from the east coast media-monopolizing Irving family) a four-station Atlantic Canada chain called CIHF-TV, also known as Maritime Independent Television (MITV). With this acquisition, Global was now broadcasting in six Canadian provinces. Asper next set his sights on Alberta and Quebec.

In 1993, and again in 1996, the CRTC put out calls for applications for television licences in Calgary and Edmonton. Canwest applied twice, and was turned down both times. The first time, the CRTC reported it hadn't received a suitable proposal from any applicant; the second time, Asper lost out to Craig Media.

Between his two CRTC applications, Asper also tried to take over Western International Communications (WIC) after the death of its founder, Frank Griffiths. WIC owned four television stations in Alberta (Calgary, Edmonton, Lethbridge, Red Deer), three in British Columbia (Vancouver, Victoria, Kelowna), one in Hamilton, Ontario, and one in Montreal, Quebec. It also owned twelve radio stations and a number of specialty TV channels, including the Family Channel and Superchannel (now called Movie Central in western Canada and the Movie Network in eastern Canada).

In 1997, having failed in his bids for WIC and the Alberta licences, Asper stepped into the Quebec market with the purchase of CKMI, a CBC affiliate in Quebec City. With the addition of a new transmitter, the English-language broadcast service soon shifted its news and operations focus to Montreal and became known as Global Quebec.

Until this point, each Canwest station had been branded individually. With the move into Quebec, the company relaunched its collective of broadcast outlets—all with the same look and logo—as Global Television Network, the name originally attached to the small group of Ontario stations Asper and his colleagues had purchased in 1974.

But the Global Television Network wasn't yet national—Alberta still eluded Asper. In 1998, he made another play for WIC, a hostile takeover effort that once again failed. This time, though, through a spate of buying and selling shares, Canwest ended up in an accidental partnership with Shaw Communications, which had by then acquired enough of WIC to make the two companies virtually equal shareholders.

"To dissolve their unintended partnership, the companies made a deal to divide the assets of WIC," wrote Marc Edge. "Canwest would get the television stations and Shaw would take the radio stations and cable channels." The deal was finalized in 2000, giv Canwest Global its Canada-wide television system at last.

It was at this point that Victoria's CHEK-TV first became connected with Canwest Global, a relationship that would last nine years.

CANWEST'S DEAL WITH WIC didn't come without its complications. The arrangement gave the media system at least two stations in the Toronto, Vancouver, central Alberta, and Montreal regions—which was forbidden by the CRTC. To remedy the problem, Canwest rebranded four of its smaller outlets as a secondary network, dubbed CH. The newly minted CH stations were Hamilton's CHCH, Red Deer's CKRD, Montreal's CJNT and Victoria's CHEK. Kelowna's CHBC was also officially a CH station, but it was never branded as such.

That still left Canwest with one station too many on BC's Lower Mainland, meaning it had to sell CKVU, its original Vancouver station. That left Canwest with WIC's BCTV, which became part of the Global Television Network, as did the former WIC stations in Edmonton, Calgary, and Lethbridge.

The same year Canwest took over the WIC television properties, it also purchased the Southam newspaper chain from Conrad Black, creating Canada's largest media conglomerate. Canwest became the first major television network in the world to own a national newspaper chain. Along with its collection of TV stations, it now owned a dozen daily newspapers and more than two hundred small newspapers and publications across the country. "The sheer magnitude of Canwest's convergence move stunned many in Canada," wrote Edge.

In fact, the Southam purchase, with its $3.2 billion price tag, may have been the beginning of the decade-long death of the Canwest media empire, suggested Steve Maich in *Maclean's*: "[The deal] marked a quantum leap forward in Canwest's prominence and influence in Canadian media, and it marked the beginning of the company's long, losing struggle against the weight of its debt. A company that owed $549 million in 1999 owed $3.8 billion by the end of 2001."

But that didn't calm Canwest's ambition. Now under the leadership of Izzy's youngest son, Leonard Asper, who had become CEO in June 1999, the company continued to amass media assets. In 2002, Canwest bought the other half-interest in the *National Post* from Hollinger International Inc. (controlled by Conrad Black). In 2003, the year Izzy Asper died, the company launched its first Canadian radio station, CJZZ-FM ("Cool FM") in Winnipeg. A year later, CKBT-FM ("The Beat") in Kitchener took to the radio airwaves. Canwest sold both these stations in 2006, the same year it bought four radio stations in Turkey. The following year, Canwest bought the American political magazine the *New Republic*.

In that same year came what Maich called the "deal that everyone will remember as [Leonard Asper's] undoing: the mind-bogglingly complex purchase of specialty channels including Showcase, the Food Network and HGTV from Alliance Atlantis." Canwest bought the specialty broadcaster—with its $2.3 billion price tag—in partnership with US investment banking firm Goldman Sachs.

By the time of this purchase, Canwest was already in financial difficulty. In 2002, two years after its Southam purchase, the company was struggling under the weight of a $4 billion debt load. While continuing to buy some media properties, Canwest began selling other companies. Newspapers in Atlantic Canada and Saskatchewan were the first to go, selling for $255 million in the summer of 2002. "The heavy debts incurred in the [Southam newspaper] deal and a slumping advertising market have taken a toll on the company's bottom line," stated a *Toronto Star* article in October of that year. "In recent months, the value of Canwest Global shares has been cut almost in half as the heavily indebted company has tried to streamline operations to pay down debt and improve its finances."

In 2003, Canwest sold thirty southern Ontario newspapers to Osprey Media Group for $193 million. In 2004, it sold partial interests in its New Zealand and Ireland broadcast outlets and divested itself of Fireworks Entertainment, a film distribution and production company it had purchased in 1998. Staff layoffs, which had begun in 2001 with the elimination of 130 positions at the *National Post*, continued in 2003 with cuts to film, television, and music critics at Canwest's daily newspapers. Layoffs continued throughout the decade until hundreds of employees had been let go. By 2005, Canwest had also eliminated nine of its foreign news bureaus, retaining just two—in Washington, DC, and London, England.

In 2007, Canwest sold the balance of its New Zealand properties for $307 million and "pulled out of the Canadian Press news co-operative to save its $4.6 million in annual dues," opting to create its own news service instead, wrote Marc Edge. That same year, private investors offered Canwest $1.4 billion for its stake in Australia's Network TEN, an offer Leonard Asper opted not to accept, believing the property was worth more.

Despite its financial strife, Canwest managed to stay afloat for the next two years, but in the end, was not able to weather the economic downturn at the end of the decade. By late 2008, Canwest remained $3.7 billion in arrears, and its stock value had dropped from a high of almost twenty dollars in 1999 (when Leonard Asper took over as CEO) to about sixty cents.

In March 2009, Canwest defaulted on US$30.4 million in interest payments; in May, Canwest LP (the newspaper division) failed to make a $10 million payment. In its efforts to keep creditors at bay, Canwest continued selling assets. In March 2009, it sold the *New Republic*. In May, it sold its Turkish radio stations. That summer, it divested itself of the E! series of stations (formerly the CH system, which included Victoria's CHEK). Despite selling these assets and securing a number of loan extensions, in October 2009, Canwest applied for creditor protection and finally sold its shares in Australia's Network TEN—for half the price Asper had been offered two years earlier. In November, Canwest ceased trading on the Toronto Stock Exchange, almost two decades after the company had first gone public in Canada.

The rise of specialty TV and the internet were partly responsible for the dire straits Canwest now found itself in. At the time, the industry was changing dramatically, with viewers abandoning conventional television in such numbers that all broadcasters in the country were feeling the pinch. In November 2008, Leonard Asper himself declared, "The conventional television revenue model continues to be challenging, and I would dare say, broken."

Add the global recession of 2008 to these industry-wide troubles, and it made for a tough time for the entire sector. Many Canadian media companies, including Corus Entertainment and Torstar Corporation, experienced significant losses when their stock prices dropped by about 50 per cent in one year. During the same time period, though, Canwest stock fell by 92 per cent.

"The plunging market, it seems, is only part of the story [for Canwest]," wrote Duncan Hood in a December 2008 issue of *Maclean's*. "The bigger problem falls under the heading of 'questionable acquisitions at high prices,' and the piles of borrowed money required to close those deals."

Peter C. Newman pointed the finger for the company's financial plight directly at founder Izzy Asper. "His last deal, the purchase by Canwest Global Communications Corp. of Conrad Black's newspaper chain, buried the Winnipeg-based company in a catacomb of debt—$4.1 billion—from which it never emerged," he wrote in *Maclean's* in April 2009. "That debt, added to later financial obligations, has dragged the entire media empire to the very brink of insolvency."

After it applied for creditor protection in October 2009, the end came quickly for Canwest. First, the company and its bankers put some of its business units, including its television division and the *National Post*, on the block. Three months later, Canwest LP, which included ten dailies and thirty-five community papers, went on the market.

The TV stations (network and specialty) were the first to go, when Canadian cable giant Shaw Communications made a $2 billion deal with Canwest in February 2010 for control of the nationwide system. Three weeks later, on March 4, 2010, Leonard Asper gave his notice, resigning as president and CEO of the company his father had founded more than three decades earlier.

The collapse of Canwest Global became a *fait accompli* in May, when a group of investors, led by *National Post* president and CEO Paul Godfrey and collectively known as Postmedia News, bought the entire collection of Canwest newspapers—including the *National Post*—for $1.1 billion. "Mr. Godfrey's financial partners are a coalition of about 20 financial institutions consisting of private-equity and hedge-fund firms," wrote Jamie Sturgeon in the *National Post*.

"Collectively, the group owned about $450 million or just under a third of Canwest Ltd. Partnership's overall debt when the newspaper chain filed for creditor protection on January 8. Instead of risking a loss on their investment, the group is betting it can turn things around."

At that point, all that remained was for the CRTC to put its stamp of approval on the transfer of Canwest Global's television assets to Shaw Communications on October 27, 2010. With that, after more than thirty-five years of financial ups and downs, legal disputes and defying the status quo, Canwest Global ceased to exist.

Canwest Global's Impact in British Columbia

Canadian television may have debuted in central Canada, but it wasn't long before British Columbia became the second region in the country to take to the airwaves. A year after the CBC launched its first two stations in 1952, the public broadcaster's Vancouver station, CBUT, went to air.

On December 1, 1956, BC's second television station, Victoria's CHEK, took its position at Channel 6 on the dial. Over the next six years, six more privately owned television stations came into the BC market—in Kamloops (CFJC), Kelowna (CHBC), Dawson Creek (CJDC), Vancouver (CHAN), Prince George (CKPG), and Terrace (CFTK).

The BC television landscape remained fairly static over the following three decades, with just a few independent ownership changes in the province's smaller centres. For example, CFCR-TV in Kamloops changed its name to CFJC in 1971, and Jim Pattison Industries Ltd. purchased the station from owner CFJC Radio Ltd. in 1987. Similarly, CKPG-TV in Prince George changed hands in 1969.

The single major shift that occurred in the Vancouver market during this thirty-five-year period was the founding of a new independent television station, CKVU, in 1976. Four companies had vied for the licence. Vancouver-based Western Approaches Ltd. won out over applications by subsidiaries of Edmonton's Allarcom, Toronto's CHUM Ltd., and Canwest.

Despite losing its bid for this new Vancouver licence, Canwest still took its first steps into the BC television market through CKVU. In 1979, to save the new station from a takeover by Allarcom, Canwest loaned

$4 million to the majority shareholder in Western Approaches—a company called DKL, owned by Vancouver TV producer Daryl Duke, writer Norman Klenman, and lawyer Gordon Lyall.

Three years later, Canwest invested another $8 million in CKVU, this time with a condition that granted Canwest an option to purchase DKL's shares at a later date. When Canwest chose to exercise that option, DKL tried to block the sale, and for two years, the two companies battled it out in court. Finally, in 1987, the Supreme Court of British Columbia ordered DKL to sell its shares to Canwest per the original agreement, finally giving Canwest majority ownership of CKVU. In April 1989, Canwest increased its ownership to 100 per cent of CKVU.

During the last decade of the twentieth century, hints of a major broadcast upheaval to come began to ripple through the TV industry in British Columbia. In 1989, WIC took full ownership of Victoria's CHEK, Vancouver's BCTV (CHAN), and Kelowna's CHBC. In 1997, Baton Broadcasting Inc. launched Vancouver's fourth conventional station, CIVT (better known as VTV). And in 1998 came the deal that would lead to Canwest's eventual acquisition of the WIC television assets, a deal that set off a domino effect in the provincial TV landscape.

When the WIC-to-Canwest transfer took effect in September 2001, every private TV station in Vancouver and Victoria changed its network affiliation. *Vancouver Sun* TV critic Alex Strachan explained the complicated transfers of ownership:

> BCTV has been renamed Global BC, and will carry Canwest Global programming.
>
> VTV has been renamed CTV British Columbia, and will carry CTV programming.
>
> Global TV has been renamed CKVU 13, and will carry CHUM/Citytv programming.
>
> And CHEK-TV has been renamed CH Victoria, and will carry Canwest Global programming . . .
>
> CTV BC general manager Robert Hurst said Vancouver and Lower Mainland viewers are going to be well-served, if confused at first. "I really don't think there's ever been

anything quite like this in Canadian broadcasting where you have four stations in one place all changing identities and affiliations in the same instant," Hurst said.

To make matters even more complicated, each station took advantage of its required rebranding to launch updated news programming. "Some newscasts have been lengthened, some shortened," wrote Strachan. "Some have moved to new times, and others are staying where they are. And some prominent local newscasters and reporters have traded places."

On top of that, to further confuse the viewing public, CHAN, or Global BC, continued to use "BCTV" in reference to its newscasts, while the former VTV dubbed itself "BC-CTV."

Within a month of this upheaval, two more pieces were added to the TV puzzle in the region when the religion-based NOW-TV and The New VI, owned by Toronto's CHUM Ltd., launched in the Fraser Valley and Victoria, respectively, both beaming into the Vancouver market.

In 2002, after the dust had settled, with all the new affiliations and newscasts in place, Canwest Global—via Global BC in Vancouver and CH Vancouver Island—was left with 70.6 per cent of the newscast market share in the Lower Mainland–Vancouver Island region. Also by this time, Canwest had acquired the Southam newspaper chain, giving it 100 per cent of the local daily newspaper market in the same region.

Canwest Global had gone from being a bit player in Canada's west coast media market to a near-monopoly. In just two years, the corporation had amassed most of the print and television outlets on the Lower Mainland and Vancouver Island, creating what the Communications, Energy and Paperworkers Union called an "unprecedented and horrifying" concentration of ownership.

Canwest Global now owned Vancouver's two daily English-language newspapers, the *Province* and the *Vancouver Sun*, along with the *Vancouver Courier* and fifteen other Vancouver-area community newspapers. In addition, it owned the *National Post* and Vancouver Island's three daily newspapers, the *Times Colonist*, the *Nanaimo Daily News*, and the *Alberni Valley Times*. Canwest also now owned BCTV, the most-watched television station in Vancouver, and Victoria's CH (formerly CHEK).

Within this short period of time, Canwest Global's single voice on the west coast had become virtually the *only* voice in what was one of the country's largest media markets. By the time that voice was silenced a decade later, it had had an impact on every private television station and almost every newspaper in the Lower Mainland–Vancouver Island region.

IF THE NEWLY EXPANDED Canwest Global empire was causing concerns over media concentration across the country, the company's near-monopoly in British Columbia was ringing alarm bells at the nation's highest policy-making and regulatory levels.

On March 19, 2003, the Senate of Canada authorized a study "to examine and report on the current state of Canadian media industries, emerging trends and developments in these industries; the media's role, rights, and responsibilities in Canadian society; and current and appropriate future policies relating thereto." It was the third federal study of news media policy in thirty-five years, following the 1970 Davey Report and the 1981 Kent Commission.

The Senate Committee issued an interim report in May 2004, with its final report released in June 2006. The goal of this latest study, wrote the committee in its final report, was "to identify ways in which federal public policy could be rethought to foster healthy, independent news media for the 21st century." In a segment of the report titled "Causes for Concern," the committee listed four items it found to be "serious problems" within the Canadian news media. Topping that list was media concentration: "Many regions and markets are characterized by high levels of concentration in news media ownership and/or cross-ownership."

The report further deconstructed the committee's findings, listing the three regions in the country where witnesses expressed the greatest worry over the integrity of the media. At the top of that list was Vancouver, followed by New Brunswick and French-language media in Quebec. "Various critics described Canwest's dominance in [the Vancouver] market as 'frighteningly powerful' and 'debilitating for voices.'"

David Beers, a former *Vancouver Sun* reporter and founder of online news site *The Tyee*, was one of more than forty witnesses who testified before the Senate Committee in Vancouver early in 2005. He expressed frustration over Canwest's dominance in the Lower Mainland:

> Vancouver is a heartbreaking place to be a dedicated news reporter, news editor, or news reader, because a single company owns the big papers, the big TV news station, and so many other media properties. There is simply not enough competition to keep that owner honest.
>
> By honest I mean dedicated to informing readers, rather than pandering to advertisers or to political allies.
>
> Other speakers today, I believe, have detailed the cost. The slashed staffs. The lowered standards. The embarrassing boosterism. The conflicts of interest. The lack of accountability to the public. The stunted civic conversation that results.
>
> But don't feel sorry for us way out here on the far edge of Canada with our peculiar situation. Feel alarm for where all of Canada may be headed, for B.C. is but an expression of today's trends. Consolidation of titles. Cross-ownership of mediums. Convergence and homogenization of content. Most of Canada will soon enough look the same if your committee isn't successful in crafting and winning a different way forward.

The *Final Report on the Canadian News Media* went on to list a number of recommendations designed to ensure media concentration of the magnitude of Canwest's domination in Vancouver would not be repeated. It advised "that a new section, dealing with mergers of news-gathering organizations, be added to the Competition Act." The committee also recommended compelling the CRTC and the Competition Bureau to come together, rather than working independently, when considering media mergers; mandating greater disclosure by media companies so consumers are clear about which companies own which media outlets; amending the Broadcasting Act to give higher priority to news and information programming; and giving the

CRTC more responsibility in the creation, monitoring and penalizing of "companies involved in cross-media mergers."

While these recommendations may or may not have, at some point, impacted what Marc Edge called Canwest's "unprecedented control of the Vancouver media," the issue became moot (with respect to Canwest) with the company's 2010 demise.

AS DISCUSSED EARLIER IN this chapter, after Canwest Global defaulted on millions of dollars in interest payments in the spring and summer of 2009, its end came quickly. By the fall of 2010, Shaw Communications owned the Global Television Network stations, and Postmedia News had snapped up all the Canwest newspapers, including the *National Post*, the *Vancouver Sun*, the *Province*, the *Times Colonist*, the *Nanaimo Daily News*, and the *Alberni Valley Times*. A year later, Postmedia sold all three daily newspapers on Vancouver Island, along with twenty BC community newspapers, to Glacier Media for $86.5 million.

As for Victoria's CHEK, Canwest put it up for sale, along with all its E! system (formerly CH) stations, in the summer of 2009. When Canwest couldn't find a buyer for CHEK, it announced it would shut the station down as of September 1, 2009. But CHEK's employees, and the Vancouver Island community, had a different idea.

four

A SHORT HISTORY OF CHEK-TV

At 11:25 Thursday night, the great moment came. Engineers flipped the switch and the Channel 6 test pattern was witnessed by Victorians who had sat up late to witness the historic event. After years of planning, disappointments and reverses, CHEK-TV was on the air.

—*Daily Colonist* (Victoria), November 30, 1956

SINCE ITS BEGINNING, VICTORIA'S CHEK-TV has been a trailblazer in the television industry in British Columbia. When it launched in 1956, it was the first television station to take to the airwaves on Vancouver Island, the first independently owned station in British Columbia and the first station in Canada with colour telecasting capabilities. A half-century later, CHEK became the first employee-owned television station in North America.

The station has gone through five ownership changes, three network affiliations, and three different names. But in 2009, it came full circle—back to its roots as a locally owned, independent television station called CHEK.

IN 1950, VICTORIA RADIO broadcaster David Armstrong launched CKDA-AM radio (with the "DA" in the call letters standing for David

CHEK IT OUT

CHEK was the first television station in Canada with the ability to broadcast in colour. But the CBC didn't make colour programming available until 1967.

For a few years in the early 1970s, CHEK's newscasts jumped back and forth between colour and black and white, creating an "unusual" viewing experience, remembers longtime reporter Bruce Kirkpatrick.

"Our studio cameras broadcast in black and white, but the news stories were shot on colour 16-mm film, which was broadcast in colour," he said. "It was unusual to see the news anchor in black and white, then a story he introduced pop up in colour."

CHEK began airing its locally produced, non-news programs in colour in 1973. ∎

Armstrong). Four years later, he was awarded British Columbia's first FM radio licence. In 1956, he made history again, when he was awarded British Columbia's first independent television licence.

On March 29, 1956, the Victoria-based *Daily Times* announced "Armstrong Gets City TV Station: CKDA Gets Licence for Channel 6." The article reported that the thirty-six-year-old had won the licence over another applicant, International Television Corp. Ltd., a New Westminster company owned by Armstrong's mentor (and CKNW radio founder), William Rea.

The licence application promised that Armstrong's new Victoria TV station would air a mix of feature films, network and syndicated shows, and local programming from 4:00 p.m. to midnight every day. Local productions would include "live programs covering the news, weather, amateur talent, panel discussions, cooking and homemaking, children's shows, medical and legal forums, fishing, hunting and hobby shows," reported the *Daily Times*.

Armstrong's partners in his new TV venture were vice-president and station manager Charlie White, a TV executive from Portland,

Oregon, who held 21 per cent of the Victoria station's shares, and Dr. Martin Mathison, a dentist from New Westminster, who also owned 21 per cent of the company and served as secretary-treasurer. As majority shareholder, Armstrong, with a 58 per cent stake, was president.

The original name of the television outlet was to be CKTV, but in the summer of 1956, Armstrong announced its new identity— CHEK-TV. Broadcast standards of the day required six-character call letters, starting with CH, CJ, or CK. Armstrong said they chose CHEK "because it lends itself to promotional ideas—for instance, 'Check Channel 6 tonight'"

In the mid-1950s, more than twenty thousand Greater Victoria households had TV sets, and viewers could choose from seven different television channels. One of the greatest challenges Armstrong and his colleagues faced in launching CHEK was convincing those viewers that the signal from this new local station would not block programming from the existing Vancouver and US broadcasters. As it turned out, in some parts of the city, the CHEK-TV signal did, in fact, interfere with a local favourite, KING 5 from Seattle. Viewers affected by this interference had to buy costly adapters to fix the problem until cable television arrived in 1960.

Another challenge faced by Armstrong's group in launching the new TV station was building a home for it. Before construction had even started, it was postponed by a change in location. Facing boiling opposition from neighbours, Armstrong and company abandoned the site they'd originally chosen in the Victoria suburb of Saanich in favour of a different Saanich location, about one kilometre to the north, on Epsom Drive.

There, they also met with disapproval from local residents, 138 of whom signed a petition stating that "the station would have a detrimental effect on values of residential properties nearby, and secondly [that] a commercial zone as proposed is neither required nor acceptable to the taxpayers in the area." Despite these objections, Saanich council unanimously approved the required rezoning for the Epsom Drive site, thus welcoming the new TV station to the community. But the new station's launch was delayed another two months because of technical and construction issues on the $90,000, two-storey, seven-thousand-square-foot studio and office facilities.

CHEK-TV finally went to air as a privately owned CBC affiliate at 5:00 p.m. on December 1, 1956. After playing "O Canada" and three half-hour episodes of established TV series (*The Count of Monte Cristo*, *The Adventures of Wild Bill Hickok*, and *Oh, Susanna*), CHEK aired thirty minutes of opening ceremonies. Joining Armstrong and White in the studio for the occasion were more than two hundred local business and government officials. At 10:00 p.m., CHEK aired its first-ever newscast, a fifteen-minute segment hosted by anchor Graham Thompson. The top story of the day was the launch of the new television station.

Within months, CHEK-TV's broadcast schedule included its first locally produced show, *TV House Party*, hosted by longtime radio deejay Norm Pringle. "The station had just opened its doors, but 'they didn't have anybody to program it,'" said Pringle in a 2002 *Times Colonist* article. "So I came up with an idea for *House Party*, where we could get various people from high schools to lip sync to the records. Some of them were so good at it, you'd think it was [the real thing]."

Over the next few years, CHEK's list of local programming expanded to include live morning and midday talk shows (*Daybreak* and *The Ida Clarkson Show*, respectively) and a dance party show for teenagers titled *Club 6*.

WHEN CHEK-TV LAUNCHED IN 1956, it also launched a new way of reporting the news on Vancouver Island. The man charged with leading the television station's news programming was Andy Stephen, who had been news director at radio station CKDA since 1953. When CHEK took its place on the TV dial, Stephen added television news director and anchor to his job description.

He worked long hours, starting his days with the 7:00 a.m. CKDA newscast, then shifting over to television, where he reported, edited, and wrote scripts all day before anchoring the dinner-hour *6 Star Final News*, CHEK's first regularly scheduled newscast.

Stephen was also a co-host of the *Noon Show* when it launched in 1957, a program he later co-hosted with Ida Clarkson. In 1961, he began a twenty-two-year run as host of a weekly political affairs show, *Capital Comment*, a venue for politicians and members of the

DANCE FEVER

When it launched in April 1962, CHEK-TV's *Club 6* became an instant hit. Within three months, the half-hour weekly show had expanded to ninety minutes, and the "club" had 3,000 members from 120 different towns and cities in Canada and the US— including 500 members in the Victoria area. Every week, about 125 teens showed up at the CHEK studios, hoping for a chance to dance on the show, but admission was limited to 20 couples. "Reservations will be made by telephone: receptionist to keep a list of teenagers and check them in each day," stated an internal production paper. "This program will do its best to give good PR to the teenagers of Victoria. To this end, they will be asked to wear ties during program . . . Age of participants should be between thirteen and nineteen years."

Producers advised the show's host, twenty-eight-year-old Bob Aylward, "to play [his role] straight, similar to Dick Clark's approach." From behind the "milk bar," Aylward was to "chat with the teenagers about the music, favourite vocalists, current dance crazes, etc. We plan to incorporate various features into the program to set us apart from dance shows running on other channels."

Originally envisioned as a television malt shop where teens danced to the music of a jukebox, the set ended up being an open dance floor, with little furniture to hinder the latest dance steps.

In addition to his *Club 6* hosting duties, Aylward presented weather forecasts on the evening news and reported for the late-night news. "You did everything really [in those days]," he said in a video prepared for CHEK's fiftieth anniversary in 2006. "If you were on the air at one point, on the next show you might run a camera, or you might run a boom microphone, you might do the lighting on the grid, or you might be the board announcer in the booth, or you might be Mr. Music and do the audio all the time." ■

BC Legislative Press Gallery to come together to discuss the issues of the day.

When Stephen had first marched into the Legislature with his crew and equipment in 1956, those same press gallery colleagues hadn't exactly welcomed him, wrote fellow legislative reporter Jim Hume in a *Times Colonist* article more than fifty years later.

> [Stephen] was the first "electronic" reporter, one who carried a microphone instead of a notebook; one who could play back a politician's quote accurately and beyond question. More than that, he would be accompanied by an assistant carrying a camera so that he could not only play back the complete words a politician was saying, but also moving pictures of them being said.
>
> It was all unthinkable to print purists—until we were invited to sit with Andy as part of the panel on his weekly TV show *Capital Comment*. We quickly learned to enjoy the extra touch of Island recognition TV exposure brought, and enjoyed it even more when *Capital Comment* went province wide.

In 1972, CHEK launched "a major expanded news department," complete with increased staff, more comprehensive local news programming, and a larger studio and newsroom. "In addition to these expanded facilities," reported the Port Hardy–based *North Island Gazette*, "CHEK has installed a new 16mm color [*sic*] film processor for rapid, same-day delivery of color film to meet the demands of color television." Modern editing equipment and cameras "will permit CHEK newsmen to go everywhere in Victoria and to present eye witness accounts at first hand."

One of the new reporters hired as part of this expansion was Bruce Kirkpatrick, who, like Stephen, had been a CKDA radio reporter before making the move to TV. Kirkpatrick started at CHEK in October 1972 and remained on the job for the next forty-one years. When he retired in May 2013, Kirkpatrick was the station's longest-serving employee.

During his four-decade career at CHEK, Kirkpatrick witnessed dramatic changes in television news production. "Doing TV news in Victoria in the early 1970s was physical," he said. "Cameras were heavy, and light was precious—cameras needed a lot of light to put images on film. Film came in 100- and 400-foot spools in shiny boxes, and it was expensive. An 'err' or an 'umm' could cost a buck as the camera rolled on."

In those days, he said, reporters would spend their mornings covering two or three stories. Then there was "the film dash—getting the film back to the station to be 'souped,' or developed. Then the film was put through a viewer and sound box and cut by hand. The reporter and cameraman would watch and give directions as each shot—an average of three seconds long—was painstakingly cut and put onto a story reel with soundbites." Because the editing process was so time-consuming, a story that happened in the afternoon wouldn't be ready for the suppertime newscast.

Today, news production is completely computerized. "It is much faster, and news deadlines can be pushed right up to airtime," said Kirkpatrick. "News is more immediate today, and with all the electronic advancements, it looks much more sophisticated and sleeker."

CHEK was also the starting point for well-known BC newscaster Pamela Martin, who went on to anchor newscasts on CTV affiliate stations in Vancouver for nearly thirty-five years—first at CHAN (better known as BCTV), then at CIVT (a.k.a. CTV-BC) after the 2001 network shuffle. Martin's first job in television, though, was as host of a lifestyle program on CHEK in 1975. She also briefly co-hosted *Daybreak* and *Barton & Co.* before succumbing to the lure of the big city on the Lower Mainland.

Arguably the biggest name to come out of CHEK is Michaela Pereira, who now sits in the news anchor chair for CNN's New York–based morning show, *New Day*. The Saskatoon native started her broadcasting career in 1994 as co-host of a local magazine show called *CHEK Around*—alongside longtime CHEK personality Gordie Tupper. After four years at the Victoria station, Pereira moved to San Francisco cable channel ZDTV, followed by nine years at *KTLA Morning News* in Los Angeles, before taking the CNN job.

VICTORIA'S FIRST LADY OF TELEVISION

Ida Clarkson, who came to be known as "Victoria's First Lady of Television," started as a copywriter at CHEK in 1961—and accidentally became a talk-show host a year later. When one of the station's *Noon Show* co-hosts quit in February 1962, producers asked Clarkson, who had a background in radio, to fill in while they searched for someone to sit in the co-host chair full-time. "Then they just never bothered to get anybody else," said Clarkson in *TV Guide* in 1981.

So began the Victoria native's thirty-year run as host of a daily talk show on CHEK. The *Noon Show* eventually became the *Ida Clarkson Show*. In 1981, it was renamed *At 11*, but was commonly known as *Ida Clarkson at 11*. It started an hour earlier to accommodate a new noon newscast. In 1984, the year the BC Association of Broadcasters named Clarkson Broadcaster of the Year, her time slot shifted to 3:00 p.m. to make room for daytime soap opera *The Young and the Restless* at 11:00 a.m.

Over the years, Clarkson occasionally had a co-host, but it was always seen as her show. And for the first fifteen years or so, it aired live, something that occasionally led to unusual television viewing. "For instance, I started the show one day and I was sitting on my microphone," said Clarkson, as quoted in *TV Guide*. "So I had to stand up, take the microphone out from underneath me, put it around my neck and go through the whole business of apologizing on the air. Another time I got a bad case of the giggles and couldn't stop. Our sewing lady had brought a pattern for a glove. And it looked rather like a cow's udder. Every time she held this thing up, I started to laugh."

Speaking of cows, Clarkson's production crew once brought a bovine guest into the studio. Her co-host at the time, Bob Willett, offered to milk the cow, something he'd never done before. He succeeded in coaxing some milk from the udders, but only after "sweet-talking" the cow live on air for several minutes.

. . . continued on next page

Then there was the time the SPCA brought in a reindeer that skewered one of Clarkson's scripts with its antler and an owl that flew into the rafters and refused to come down.

For Clarkson, the highlight was a 1962 episode on which Victor Borge appeared, unannounced, in the middle of a live broadcast. The legendary musical comedian, who was in town to perform at a local arena, had been invited to be a guest on Clarkson's show—but had declined. On a whim, he showed up anyway, disrupting the show in the best way possible.

In 1981, *TV Guide* writer Paul Grescoe described Clarkson's show:

> She wears sensible dresses and round glasses and sits with her legs crossed, a clipboard of notes perched on her lap. The set looks like a suburban living-room: flowers on a coffee table and books and bric-a-brac artistically arranged on wicker shelves. "The show is not controversial," Clarkson says. "I don't think people should be disturbed during their lunch hour."

Clarkson retired from CHEK in 1991, and died in 2012 at age eighty-five. In a *Times Colonist* article, longtime CHEK reporter Bruce Kirkpatrick remembered her as a woman who "started in broadcast journalism when it was a man's domain." At Clarkson's memorial, Kirkpatrick again honoured his pioneering colleague: "She meant a lot for women in broadcasting in Victoria." ∎

FOR TELEVISION VIEWERS IN the 1950s, it may have appeared all was well with CHEK-TV. But behind the scenes, things were rocky right from the beginning. Within a year of the station taking to the airwaves, Charlie White and Martin Mathison were already out of the picture. Ironically, White, who left because of a dispute with Armstrong, sold his shares in the company to Bill Rea, who had been Armstrong's competitor in the bid for the Victoria licence in 1956.

Armstrong retained the majority of the shares, but by the turn of the decade, he and the station were losing money. In 1963, CHEK changed hands for the first time when Armstrong sold his stake in the company to British Columbia Television, owner of Vancouver's CHAN, a station better known today as BCTV.

By that time, CTV was a national network, and BCTV was its westernmost station. CHEK was still a CBC affiliate, but when British Columbia Television purchased the controlling interest in CHEK, the two stations began sharing programming. CHEK became a sort of cross-affiliate, presenting a mixture of CTV, CBC, and locally produced shows. Over the years, CHEK's CTV content increased, until January 1981 when the station disaffiliated with CBC and became a full-time CTV broadcaster.

A 1980 *Media West* article further explained the transition: "When CHEK first went on air, it was the first station in Victoria, which meant that it had to carry CBC signals. In Victoria, the plan to establish a CBC station on Channel 10 for Vancouver Island one year ago [1979] left CHEK free to drop its CBC signal. Plans for the CBC station fell through, but the CRTC [had already] approved the move by CHEK to the CTV."

As CHEK was transitioning from CBC to CTV in the 1970s, CTV was gradually adding rebroadcast transmitters up and down Vancouver Island and on the Lower Mainland. That meant when CHEK finally became a full CTV affiliate, its coverage area had expanded to include most of the Island and the Lower Mainland as far as the town of Hope, about 150 kilometres northeast of Vancouver.

The same year CHEK joined the CTV network, Frank Griffiths (Vancouver entrepreneur and then-owner of the Vancouver Canucks hockey team) founded WIC (Western International Communications Ltd.). A year later, in 1982, WIC bought controlling interest in British Columbia Television, eventually taking full ownership of the company, including BCTV and CHEK, in 1989.

Under WIC's ownership, CHEK expanded its operations into its current studios on Kings Road, close to downtown Victoria. The multi-million dollar building had originally been constructed for the CBC, but when the national public broadcaster failed to establish a Victoria television station, CHEK took over the new facility in December 1983. CHEK started broadcasting from the new locale in September 1984.

The move to the "ultra-modern" three-level facility was "a dream come true for CHEK-TV," wrote Alyn Edwards in *Broadcaster* magazine in December 1984. CHEK had long since outgrown its space on Epsom Drive, he said, "with staffers stashed in portable trailers, contrived mezzanine space and leased downtown offices."

Then-news director Tony Cox said the move from a small, outdated building overlooking a suburban golf course into the station's new, modern, urban digs "has just created a complete change of attitude. We're doing two and three live interviews every day now . . . Better working conditions mean better stories. The employees are even dressing better. They have gotten away from that sort of country cousin attitude."

The larger facilities allowed CHEK to expand on many levels and, for the next decade, the station thrived, with staff numbers peaking at 120 and locally produced programming on the rise. But soon after WIC founder Frank Griffiths died in 1994, things started to crumble for the parent company. While two high-powered media families fought for control of WIC, Canwest Global lobbed its first takeover attempt, as described by Reuters in November 1995:

> Canadian broadcaster Canwest Global Communications Corp. launched a C\$636 million takeover bid Monday [November 13, 1995] for WIC Western International Communications Ltd., which would form Canada's largest private television network.
>
> WIC has been the subject of takeover rumours for months as two families battled for control of the lucrative Vancouver, British Columbia-based broadcast empire . . .
>
> WIC has been the centre of a lengthy ownership dispute between the family of Dr. Charles Allard and relatives of WIC's late founder Frank Griffiths.
>
> In April 1994, the Allard family offered to buy a controlling stake in WIC's voting shares from an ailing Griffiths. The offer was rejected and the Allards sued, arguing their offer triggered a provision which would convert non-voting shares into voting stock.

The battle over WIC continued for the next four years until, through a series of financial transactions, failed partnerships, and court cases, Canwest Global and Shaw ended up as co-owners of the company. To dissolve their unwanted partnership, they split WIC in two—with Canwest taking the television assets (including CHEK) and Shaw taking the radio and specialty stations.

The lengthy battle for WIC did not leave CHEK untouched. In 1997, new competition in the Vancouver market—in the form of Baton Broadcasting's just-launched VTV—led WIC to cut costs, leaving CHEK without a late-night newscast and more than twenty employees out of work. Before the CRTC put its final stamp of approval on the Canwest/Shaw arrangement in 2000, another nine CHEK employees were laid off. In the three years leading up to its affiliation with Global, CHEK had lost almost 30 per cent of its workforce, bringing staff numbers down to about eighty.

Canwest Global's acquisition of WIC's assets also precipitated some major shifts in the British Columbia television landscape. Because CHEK's signal reached into Vancouver, where Canwest already owned CKVU and had just acquired BCTV, and because the CRTC forbids multiple television stations in a single market, CHEK had to change. In 2001, the station was rebranded as part of a secondary television system called CH. Similarly, television outlets in Hamilton, Red Deer, and Montreal took on the CH logo. (Kelowna's CHBC, officially part of the CH system, was not rebranded, retaining its original call letters.)

For forty-five years, the television station in Victoria had been CHEK in one form or another—CHEK-TV, chek 6, CHEK 6, chek SIX, chek TELEVISION VANCOUVER ISLAND, or just plain CHEK—but in September 2001, CHEK was no more. The station's name became CH Vancouver Island.

A month later came another shake-up for the Victoria broadcaster when, for the first time in its history, it was no longer the only station on Vancouver Island. On October 4, 2001, Toronto's CHUM Limited launched The New VI, one of six stations (the only one outside of Ontario) in its fresh-faced NewNet system. With its glassy, open-concept, high-tech studios in downtown Victoria and its "hip, youthful" style, The New VI meant competition for viewership and advertising dollars. For the first time, CHEK (now CH) would have to fight for its place in the market, as Mike Devlin wrote in the *Times Colonist* in September 2001:

The launch [of The New VI] will mark more than the birth of a new station. It will kick off a classic fight for viewers and advertising dollars between stations with two different schools of thought.

On one side will be CH, formerly CHEK-TV, Victoria's only commercial television station since 1956, which comes armed with solid programming and years of hard-won credibility. Facing it will be The New VI, offering a flashy, vibrant, youthful style.

Shrinking TV audiences and a weakening economy should make it a difficult battle, but both sides say they're ready . . .

CH recently repackaged itself to meet the challenges of a new competitor and the battle for advertising. The New VI will need to make a dent in CH's longstanding reputation.

Today, the station formerly known as The New VI is called CTV Two Vancouver Island and is part of Bell Media's secondary CTV Two system.

WHEN CHEK BECAME CH in 2001, Canwest "went on a hiring spree—spending its CRTC mandated community benefits," wrote the station's news director Rob Germain in a 2012 email:

A VP of Canwest famously said, at the re-launch party when CHEK was rebranded as CH, that he had a "trunk full of money," and he was going to spend most of in Victoria. At first, they did. Canwest hired a lot [of staff] in news and they created *Go! Magazine* [a half-hour lifestyle show]. Three years later, when the community benefits commitment was over, Canwest started to lay off [staff] and consolidate many of our departments.

First they laid off our master control staff—of more than a dozen. Master control was moved to Calgary. Then they eliminated our traffic department (which schedules programs and commercials). Traffic went to Toronto. Then they got rid of our payroll and HR departments. (Those functions would be done out of Winnipeg/Burnaby.) There were numerous small cuts to news and other departments along the way—and many vacancies that were never filled.

Still, at its fiftieth anniversary party in 2006, CH made it clear to Vancouver Islanders that, despite the name change, the newly installed competition, and the recent cuts, the station was here to stay.

But that didn't mean there weren't more changes to come.

In September 2007, all the stations in the CH system took on yet another new name—E!—when they became affiliated with the US-based E! Entertainment Television Network, a multinational producer and distributor of entertainment and lifestyle programming.

For the Victoria station, this meant a youth-focused programming schedule filled with trendy celebrity gossip, reality, and entertainment shows. At the same time, its newscast returned to something familiar to older viewers—it was renamed *CHEK News*, the name by which it had been known for its first forty-five years. "It's what people know us as best," said Rob Germain in the *Times Colonist*. "For a long time, people have called us *CHEK News*, even when we were CH."

In the end, the station's stint as E! was short-lived. The impact of its parent company's financial crisis started to show up in Victoria late in 2008, when the station's commercial production department was cut, its general manager let go, and its control room operations—along with those of Canwest stations in Montreal, Winnipeg, and Kelowna—consolidated and shifted to Vancouver. Countrywide, Canwest laid off about 5 per cent of its workforce that November, a move designed to save the company $61 million a year. At CHEK, nineteen employees lost their jobs, leaving a local workforce of just forty employees.

"We announced a number of difficult but necessary changes, to make sure that we set up ourselves for long-term viability and success here at CHEK," said Global BC vice-president Brett Manlove in a *Times Colonist* article.

But that success wasn't destined to happen under Canwest management. As the company's fortunes continued to fail through the winter of 2008–2009, Canwest made an announcement that would further unsettle the Victoria broadcaster. In a February 5, 2009, press release, Canwest announced it was "exploring strategic options" for its five E! stations. "The sale of the stations is one of several options being considered by the company." Other options included reprogramming the stations or closing them down.

For staff at CHEK, the "threat of closure was devastating," reported producer Dana Hutchings in the 2010 documentary *Reality CHEK: Covering News and Making History*. Operations manager Bill Pollock said: "I remember going home that night thinking, 'What am I going to do with the rest of my life? This is all I've ever done.'" Canwest reassured staff it would find a buyer for the station.

Four months later, Canwest announced it had found a buyer—but not for CHEK. Independent Toronto-based broadcaster Channel Zero had agreed to buy the E! system stations in Hamilton and Montreal, and within a few weeks Canwest announced it would absorb CHBC in Kelowna into its main Global television network.

For CHEK and Red Deer's CHCA, the news wasn't so positive. On July 22, 2009, Canwest announced the two stations would be closed as of August 31 because the financially strapped corporation had failed to find buyers for them. About forty staff members in Victoria received layoff notices that day.

"We recognize that today's decision is difficult not only on the employees and their families, but on the community that has been served for a long time by [CHEK]," said John Douglas of Canwest, as quoted the next day in the *Times Colonist*. He added that there were no "viable options" for keeping the station running.

Canwest may not have come up with any viable options, but its employees did. Backed by a swell of community support, the staff at CHEK refused to let the station fade to black. "If we were going to go down, we were going to go down with a huge fight, and whether we had the community behind us or what, we really believed in what we were doing," said Pollock in the *Reality CHEK* documentary.

After what was later referred to in media reports as "a tough three weeks of roller coaster rides" and "marathon negotiations," the employees at CHEK no longer worked for the station—they owned it.

five

REFUSING TO FADE TO BLACK

Local does matter to audiences. People do want to read about and see what is happening in their communities, yet newspapers and TV in Canada have largely forgotten that as they replaced specialists with generalists and stopped covering things like school boards and much of municipal government and in most cases have even abandoned putting reporters at provincial legislatures.

—**Christopher Waddell,** *Policy Options* magazine, 2009

WHEN CANWEST GLOBAL ACQUIRED CHEK as part of the WIC television package it purchased in 2000, things got off to a good start. "It was good times for the first little while," said CHEK news director Rob Germain. Like all corporations that buy TV stations, Canwest was required, as a condition of licence, to offer up a package of "community benefits" when it bought CHEK. In this case, the CRTC ordered Canwest to spend 10 per cent of the purchase price of the station in the community.

To spend that money, the new corporate owner hired staff and created new programming. "Then, what we called 'the WIC benefits' got spent," said Germain. "We started to get clawbacks . . . we started to see consolidation." Various departments at CHEK— master control, traffic, programming, human resources, and payroll—joined centralized Canwest Global operations in other parts of the country.

"One thing after another was consolidated," said Germain. "In February of 2009, they got rid of our commercial production department. We couldn't produce any local commercials . . . We were left with newsgathering, a very small sales team, executive offices, operations and engineers. We were no longer a stand-alone station. We couldn't operate without a network."

On February 5, 2009, Canwest announced plans to divest itself of CHEK along with the four other stations in its E! system—Red Deer's CHCA, Hamilton's CHCH, Kelowna's CHBC, and Montreal's CJNT. The stations were to be "sold, rebranded, reprogrammed or closed, depending on the outcome of a review," stated a 2009 *Times Colonist* article. For Germain, "in some ways, it was welcome news, because it couldn't get any worse."

At first, Canwest executives assured CHEK staff they would find a buyer for the station. "They told us all along that there were people kicking the tires and expressing interest," said Germain.

One potential buyer was Toronto's Channel Zero, an independent broadcaster that originally considered buying all five E! network outlets. Ultimately, it opted to take just the two stations closest to Toronto—Hamilton's CHCH and Montreal's CJNT (which it renamed Métro 14 Montréal and sold to Rogers Media three years later). "Initially, it was appealing to Canwest to sell all the stations to one purchaser, and we were quite prepared to do that on the right terms," said Channel Zero CEO Cal Millar in a 2012 interview.

By early May, though, Millar and his colleagues had decided not to purchase the three western stations in the E! network. In addition to the prohibitive distance from Channel Zero's head office, Canwest had already largely dismantled the Victoria, Kelowna, and Red Deer properties, meaning any purchaser would, in effect, have to rebuild them, he said:

At CHCH, they hadn't done that. [Canwest] hadn't gotten around to it, and they had stopped doing capital investments, so they weren't proceeding with it. So CHCH was sitting there with

TELEVISION 101: COMMUNITY BENEFITS

Beginning in 1989, the CRTC required that all broadcasters that merged with or acquired other broadcast outlets "propose a specific package of significant and unequivocal benefits that will yield measurable improvements to the communities served by the broadcasting undertaking and to the Canadian broadcasting system." Generally, the larger the scope of the merger or acquisition, the greater the value of the community benefits package required to demonstrate the transaction is in the best interests of the public.

Expenses considered to be part of the normal cost of doing business for a broadcaster—such as purchasing buildings, replacing transmitters, and employee training—don't count. Nor does increasing staff, unless the hiring is directly related to new initiatives. However, projects relating to promoting Canadian talent, creating new programming, or donating money or free airtime to community organizations are in keeping with the CRTC's goals.

For example, when the CRTC approved the merger between Bell and Astral Media in the summer of 2013, it ordered the new conglomerate to pay $246.9 million in "tangible benefits" for Canadians. These benefits included funding new, independent television productions in both official languages, supporting Canadian film festivals, promoting media literacy, contributing to the Canadian Broadcast Standards Council, financing media training and development, and expanding consumer participation in Canadian broadcasting.

Often what happens with community benefits, as CHEK experienced when Canwest purchased the WIC television stations in 2000, is that the money flows for a few years, but once the community benefit commitments have been fulfilled, cutbacks begin. ∎

a fully functional studio/control room, which we could just plug into our master control in Toronto. So we unplugged [CHCH from] Canwest Calgary master control and plugged it into ours. We had a few hiccups, but we never really missed a beat . . .

In the case of CHEK, CHBC and Red Deer . . . to keep them rolling, a purchaser would have to find a way to get remote studio control, which we didn't have. We just looked at it and said, "that's going to be really hard."

Even though Channel Zero decided to pass on purchasing CHEK, Millar said he recognized the station for the "gem" it was. "If there was a station we would have loved to have bought, it was Victoria, because it was so similar to the Hamilton–Toronto market, the way Victoria works with Vancouver. CHEK can serve Victoria as local, and it can also serve Vancouver when it does primetime programming."

Because of that potential—and because of the enthusiasm, conviction, and commitment of CHEK's employees—Channel Zero didn't walk away from the Victoria station entirely. The two companies would work together and cross paths many times during the next several years.

Channel Zero may have been the largest organization to ponder buying CHEK, but at least three other groups also considered making proposals. One was a group out of Kelowna, which declined to be interviewed for this book. Another potential purchaser was longtime BCTV news anchor Tony Parsons. "I considered making a bid, but I didn't actually do it," he said a few years later. "I thought it was worthwhile saving the station if I could get a number of people together and do it . . . I talked to a number of people who I thought would be moneyed enough to be a part of it, but I didn't find a lot of enthusiasm. So I let it go."

Meanwhile, "Canwest got a whiff of what I was thinking about," he said. "I heard back—through the grapevine, not directly—that they would not consider a bid from me in any case."

That same grapevine passed the word that all parties interested in buying CHEK would be "dissuaded by Canwest," said Germain.

But according to Canwest documents, there was one buyer who was given "an exclusive period of negotiation to make an offer for

CHEK, [a period that] expired without the receipt of any offer." That potential purchaser was CHEK management.

CHEK general manager John Pollard said that, in the spring of 2009, he and a colleague considered buying the Victoria TV station. To study the feasibility of the purchase, Pollard first signed a non-disclosure agreement with Canwest so he could take a look at the books. "I had access to everything, so I could see where they were, what they'd done, and what had been happening over the past few years," he said. "I could understand there were some huge financial issues."

He and his accountant, Rod Munro, "put together a number of business plans and a number of programming options. The best we could come up with was a first-year loss of $2.5 million, which didn't make any sense because we didn't have $2.5 million to lose . . . At that point, it didn't look good."

Pollard and Munro had based their proposals on a traditional television model—local news and in-house productions slotted into a schedule filled with purchased programming. When they realized this wouldn't work financially, they dropped the idea of becoming TV station owners, holding out hope that another purchaser would come along.

But in early May, just days after Channel Zero passed on purchasing CHEK, Pollard said he "found out there were no suitors, there was nobody buying the station." During a conference call, a Global BC sales manager asked Pollard how much of CHEK's pre-booked fall advertising could be shifted to Global BC in Vancouver. To Pollard, that meant Canwest executives knew that, come fall, CHEK wouldn't need any advertising—but they didn't want to forfeit the revenue CHEK already had on the books.

"That was a 'holy shit' moment for me," said Pollard. "[I said] what do you mean? What happened to all these buyers that were lined up?" At that moment, it seemed "the whole world was coming to an end. I was in shock."

Pollard immediately went into action, meeting with representatives from other television stations to see if there was a way CHEK could link up with them and their programming. As he was researching "about a million different scenarios" and liaising with other station managers, news director Rob Germain was working on a plan of his own.

MEANWHILE, WHEN CHCH-TV STAFF in Hamilton, Ontario, heard the news in February 2009 that their workplace might be sold, they immediately came up with a proposal to buy it for themselves. A *Globe and Mail* article reported on the employees' idea:

> A group of employees, including news anchor Donna Skelly, are trying to cobble together a plan to buy the station. The proposal . . . would see the station operated as a local news and variety station, stripping out all of the U.S. programming that makes up prime time . . .
>
> The proposal is based on operating the station much like the CFL's Saskatchewan Roughriders, which are community-owned . . . "Why not come up with a radical model, and not have to generate a massive profit, simply cover our costs," Ms. Skelly said. "It is radical, but it's better than what is there now."

The idea was that CHCH's 120 employees would join with members of the community to buy and run the fifty-five-year-old station. They would reduce ad rates, so more local businesses could afford to advertise, and they would apply for funding through the CRTC's new Local Programming Improvement Fund (LPIF), a $100 million annual program designed to boost community content in small- to mid-sized markets.

Skelly suggested this community-ownership concept "could be the new model for local television." But it wasn't meant to be in Hamilton. On June 30, Canwest Global announced that Toronto-based Channel Zero had purchased CHCH, along with CJNT in Montreal.

Under this plan, the two stations would run news programming all day, switching to Movieola and Silver Screen Classics, which Channel Zero owned, during prime time. It was a concept similar to the one Skelly and her coworkers had proposed. On the day of the announcement, Skelly was quoted in the *Globe and Mail*, saying she applauded the Channel Zero programming model as "a fresh approach" and acknowledged that her staff buyout plan had "lacked the funds to get the deal done."

Skelly's proposal may not have worked for Hamilton, but it provided inspiration for CHEK news director Rob Germain, who was working on an idea to save the station in Victoria. The same day Channel Zero announced its purchase of the two stations in central Canada, Germain made a pitch, via email, to Canwest:

> I was interested to see CHCH is planning an All News/All Day format.
>
> I know Global has intentions of launching its own all-news channel in BC. The plan, I understand, is to make it a specialty channel so it would earn fee-for-carriage revenue. But with the CRTC's anticipated initiatives aimed at improving the bottom line of small and medium market TV, it may now make more sense for Global BC to launch its 24 hr. news on conventional—specifically CHEK, CHBC, CKPG [Prince George] and CFJC [Kamloops].

Germain included CKPG and CJFC, independent stations owned by the Jim Pattison Broadcast Group, in his twenty-four-hour news channel proposal because they were already running some Canwest programming at the time. Add in those two outlets, he said, and "you've got a network of stations with 24-hour news all around the province."

Germain laid out a number of "significant benefits" to his all-news plan: It would increase the "dominance" of Global News throughout the province while maintaining existing audiences. It would require no new infrastructure. Salespeople could sell ads to a province-wide network. It would eliminate all non-news programming costs. Perhaps most importantly, wrote Germain, this plan "saves local news in four markets! (Got to be worth some goodwill with the public and CRTC)."

In addition, he outlined a 5:00 a.m.-to-midnight "proposed schedule for the Global all-news channel," filled with full-length local and national newscasts, regional magazine shows, and "news wheels," or pre-recorded fifteen-minute packages of provincial news headlines that would repeat four times an hour and would run between the news and magazine programming.

FEE FOR CARRIAGE

Under the current television broadcast system in Canada, cable and satellite providers are permitted to pick up the broadcast signals of local, private television stations—without paying for them—and rebroadcast them to consumers. Since 2006, Canada's private, or "over-the-air," broadcasters have lobbied to change this. They argue that as the conventional television industry continues to struggle because of the advent of the internet and declining ad revenues, the cable companies' access to local TV signals should evolve. In short, the cable and satellite providers should have to pay a "fee for carriage," as they do for specialty channels.

American cable and satellite providers pay for content of television networks such as NBC, ABC, and CBS, helping those networks, in turn, to offset declining advertising revenues. Canadian broadcasters want a similar system. Cable companies say if they have to pay to bring local TV to Canadians, they will have to up their rates. Viewers will ultimately pay the price.

In October 2009, Canada's major broadcasters launched a campaign called "Local TV Matters," designed to let TV viewers know they'd risk losing their local television stations if cable companies didn't start paying up. The major cable and satellite companies launched a counter-campaign called "Stop the TV Tax," to let consumers know that if the cable companies had to pay fees for carriage, they would pass on the cost to consumers.

In November 2009, the CRTC, which had twice rejected the fee-for-carriage concept, held further hearings on the subject. This time, the CRTC sided with the private broadcasters, but the cable companies appealed to the Supreme Court of Canada. The question in the appeal was not whether fees for carriage should be implemented. Rather, the Supreme Court was charged with deciding whether the CRTC had the right to make that call. In December 2012, the high court ruled that the CRTC did not have

. . . continued on next page

the authority to make the decision, effectively shutting down the broadcasters' efforts to adopt a fee-for-carriage system.

That's not to say fee-for-carriage has been ruled out completely. But it means the broadcasters have to go back to the drawing board and find another avenue, and a different federal agency, to pursue the subject. ∎

In a 2012 interview, Germain explained his thought process in proposing the all-news format:

I was aware that Canwest was going to spend about $3 million to close the station . . . to pay severance and all that. And they were getting a black eye for closing the station—there was lots of media coverage about it, and nobody was happy with Canwest about it.

And so I thought there are good reasons why they may want to keep [CHEK]. But the main problem with the financials at the station, and the reason it was losing money, was because of the incredible programming cost for the primetime programming . . .

On the news side . . . we were breaking even pretty much. But now there was this chance of an LPIF coming on board, and I thought they could somehow take advantage of that [and] reduce their primetime programming costs . . .

So I started thinking about a model, and in fact, CHCH Hamilton was looking at creating a model of all-day news up until 8 o'clock, and then movies in the evening and late-night after that. So I was looking at that as a model and I was thinking well, maybe *we could do all-news*.

Rather than creating an all-news specialty channel, it made more sense to Germain for Global to change the format at existing conventional television stations: "If you want to have a 24-hour news channel for Global BC, you could have one right away, as of September, if you just make CHEK the 24-hour channel."

Germain knew there was a chance the CRTC would block the proposal because, when Canwest purchased CHEK and BCTV from WIC in 2000, it guaranteed the two stations would not share more than 10 per cent of their programming. This twenty-four-hour news channel would likely compromise that agreement, but Germain believed Canwest and the CRTC could work something out "to ease those restrictions." He figured they would cross that bridge when they came to it, so he persisted with his idea.

At first, the all-news plan "didn't get a lot of response" from the Canwest executives, so Germain and Pollard worked together to revamp it. They revised revenue and expenditure figures while putting greater emphasis on weather reports in the program schedule. They sent an updated "All-News & Weather Proposal" to Canwest on July 11.

At that point, "they appeared to be seriously looking at it," said Germain. "But at the same time, the longer things went on, and the closer we got to August 31, I knew that we needed to probably come up with a contingency plan."

Pollard was less optimistic. He believes that, by then, Canwest had already made a decision to "shut the place down, and that's what was going to happen. [They] were not interested in keeping it open."

Either way, CHEK's management team started working on a Plan B, reaching out to community leaders for support.

THE FIRST PERSON GERMAIN contacted for assistance and advice was Victoria lawyer Michael O'Connor, former chair of the CHEK Community Advisory Board and "a big high roller in the community." Founded in 2001 as one of Canwest's community commitments when it purchased CHEK from WIC, the Community Advisory Board lasted for about five years, but "ended up dissolving as soon as [Canwest was] able to dissolve it," said Germain. Even though O'Connor hadn't been involved with CHEK since the board's demise, Germain knew he was a friend of the station and might be able to help. "We needed to find a lifeline, so I phoned Michael to see if there were possible investors who were interested in backing or buying a station for a dollar and helping us run it."

CHCH: MODEL TV

In the summer of 2009, when Channel Zero bought Hamilton's CHCH-TV, media analysts quoted in the Hamilton *Spectator* hailed the station's proposed hyper-local programming model as "radical" and "a template for how local television should be done." They said it was time for the accepted television model to change—and CHCH might just lead the way.

"Conventional media operates under certain perceived constraints. Channel Zero is coming in doing things unheard of," said technology and media analyst Carmi Levy. "It's an interesting business model—exploiting the local news angle, cutting costs and putting movies in at night."

Six weeks after the station launched its new format, Levy commented again in the *Spectator*, saying he liked what he'd seen so far. He particularly liked that the station had hired fifteen more employees:

> In Levy's analysis, the new owners of the Hamilton station are making the right decision by adding staff and resources to the local news operation when many other outlets are taking them away.
>
> "For the most part, it looks like it has been business as usual with no substantial job losses," he said. "New resources are being devoted to content where others are taking them away, so I expect the results to be quite positive. The new owners seem to have a much better sense of how to build a viable local organization."

The *Spectator* also reported a thumbs up from another media watcher, Toronto's Alan Sawyer, who said CHCH's reach into Toronto, along with its command of the Golden Horseshoe area (the western end of Lake Ontario), gave it a fighting chance at long-term survival. "The breadth of its distribution might just make

. . . continued on next page

it viable. It's a hybrid local-national operation and in a market like Hamilton, that's a workable model."

It's a model that appeals to viewers *and* advertisers, he said. For example, "a local car dealer can't afford [ad] time on a Toronto station, even at the lower end. I think [advertisers] are going to come back to local television because CHCH's rates are going to be lower than any Toronto station. I think this experiment has potential, and it's going to be fascinating to watch over the next year or so."

Five years later, CHCH airs an unheard of 83.5 hours a week of local content (almost double its local content in the CanWest days). "Local works for us," said Channel Zero CEO Cal Millar. "It's not like a loss leader or a penance we have to pay. It works for us. It leads audiences into the day. We do a lot of news because it works."

But Millar said he "bristles" when he hears CHCH hailed as a new model for local television, "because I don't think any of us really know enough about the business to say, yes this is the perfect solution. I think there are certain unique aspects to certain situations, whether it's the Hamilton-Toronto market or the Vancouver-Victoria market. But I'm not sure 'poster child for local television' is exactly it. You have to take a lot of other things into consideration . . .

"Vancouver and Toronto are Canada's biggest markets, so just because something works in Hamilton because of its proximity to Toronto and in Victoria because of its proximity to Vancouver, doesn't mean it's going to work in Brandon, Manitoba, where a station closed [in 2009]. There are no guarantees that that same model would work [in other cities] because they are different businesses and different markets. So what works for our market may not work there."

So far, the local focus is working at CHCH. The station has hired more than fifty new employees over the past five years, and ad sales continue to be strong. "We're good. We've been making money for a long time," said Millar.

Having said that, CHCH, like other mid-market stations, had to do some financial juggling when it suddenly lost crucial dollars

. . . continued on next page

in the first wave of LPIF cuts in the fall of 2012. CHCH's annual LPIF grant was about $5 million, meaning it unexpectedly lost $1.7 million in the 2012–13 broadcast season, and another $1.7 million the following year. The LPIF has now been completely phased out.

But CHCH is "faring fine" in the wake of the fund's demise, said Millar. "The loss of the LPIF hasn't made it easier, but we are still growing and doing fine."

The bottom line, he said, is that a television station is a business that has to earn money. And while CHCH's hyper-local model may not be the "poster child" for television everywhere, it's "a good little business" for him and his Channel Zero colleagues. "We couldn't be happier with what we've been able to accomplish." ∎

After initial discussions with O'Connor, Germain sent him a modified version of the original all-news proposal—a version in which CHEK would be independent of Canwest and would rely, instead, on community investors for financial assistance. In a July 16 email, he asked O'Connor if he would consider leading this group of investor-owners.

A few days after Germain sent this note, Canwest senior vice-president Chris McGinley arrived at the TV station bearing bad news. On July 22, at a 9:00 a.m. meeting with CHEK management and union president Richard Konwick, she announced that Germain and Pollard's all-news proposal had been rejected, and there were no other buyers to be found. CHEK, along with CHCA in Red Deer, would go off the air as of August 31, 2009. Two hours later, McGinley met with all staff to announce the closure and issue layoff notices.

Later that day, Canwest spokesman John Douglas told a *Times Colonist* reporter the company had "tried hard to improve CHEK's profitability or to find a buyer for the station. 'But the reality is that those stations [CHEK and Red Deer] have had significant losses and were simply not able to continue on.'"

At the time, CHEK was losing about $1 million a month. "It hasn't climbed out of the red in the past decade," wrote Canadian Press

THE LPIF

In 2008, the CRTC initiated the Local Programming Improvement Fund (LPIF) "to support and improve the quality of local television programming," particularly news and information programming, in markets having fewer than one million people. The original idea was that cable and satellite service providers would contribute 1 per cent of their gross annual revenues (from the previous year's broadcast activities) to finance the $60 million fund. Eligible television stations, including private and CBC outlets, were to use their shares of the money to create new locally produced programs, and the fund was to be divided 60–40 between English- and French-language programming.

Given the economic climate of the day, by the time it implemented the LPIF in the 2009–2010 broadcast year, the CRTC had already upped the cable and satellite providers' contributions to 1.5 per cent of gross broadcasting revenues, bringing the fund's total to $102 million. In addition, it waived the requirement that eligible stations use the money for incremental programming, realizing the economic downturn meant many of the broadcasters needed the financial cushioning for operating or other existing costs.

As part of the LPIF policy, the CRTC was to conduct "a comprehensive review of the LPIF in the third year of the fund's operation [to] determine whether the fund should be maintained, modified or discontinued." That review began on April 16, 2012, with the CRTC's decision delivered three months later. In short, the commission announced it would phase out the LPIF over the following two broadcast years, discontinuing it entirely by September 1, 2014. ■

reporter James Keller, paraphrasing Douglas, who "offered several reasons why CHEK hasn't turned a profit. He said the amount of competition in Victoria has meant there isn't enough advertising revenue to go around, and he noted the station has operated in the shadow of much larger markets in Vancouver and Seattle."

Germain and Pollard didn't buy those arguments. CHEK's Richard Konwick recalled Pollard's reaction when McGinley broke the news of the station closure to management that morning:

He was getting more and more red-faced. He was getting angry. At the meeting, John was standing behind Chris McGinley, and as she was going on and on about how they were going to close the station, I could see him shaking his head. I thought that was odd. When she finished, John said, "Well thanks, Chris, but we're not closing the station. We're going to find a buyer, and we're going to keep it open."

Germain, too, refused to accept Canwest's decision. Within an hour of McGinley's management briefing, before the rest of the staff had even heard the news, he made an urgent call to potential investor O'Connor. "I let him know what was going on, that the station was going to be shut down, [that Canwest] had rejected this other format," he said. "But I felt it was still possible."

O'Connor remembered Germain and Pollard from his days on the CHEK Community Advisory Board. "I was impressed with the way they ran the station," he said. "When Rob contacted me and said would I be interested, I said yes I would." Having been raised in Victoria, O'Connor also had a personal connection to the station. "I remember the day CHEK-TV came on the air . . . I watched CHEK with my parents—the local news and sports—so I sort of grew up with CHEK-TV long before it was owned by Canwest."

O'Connor agreed to meet with Germain and Pollard the following day, and he invited "a great friend . . . and outstanding business guy, Tom Harris from Nanaimo," to join them. Germain and Pollard would have forty-five minutes to make their pitch to the pair of potential investors.

"This was our window of opportunity," said Germain.

At the July 23 meeting, Harris brought forward an idea that had, in fact, been tossed around by a number of CHEK employees since February, when Canwest had first announced its plans to divest itself of the TV station. "He suggest[ed] he may be interested in being part of an investor group that would back employees in a purchase of the station," said Germain. It was a concept inspired by the employees at a Nanaimo pulp mill called Harmac.

IN THE SPRING OF 2008, Oregon-based lumber giant Pope & Talbot declared bankruptcy after almost 160 years in business, closing seven British Columbia mills in the process. Employees in Castlegar, Grand Forks, Midway, Fort St. James, Nakusp, and Mackenzie suddenly found themselves out of work. At the Harmac Pulp Mill, which had operated near Nanaimo on Vancouver Island for sixty years, 530 people lost their jobs.

At the time of its closure, Harmac had been producing 400,000 metric tonnes of pulp every year. As one of Canada's largest pulp-producers, it ran three production lines and sold its products around the world.

The mill was profitable, and its workers saw potential. Within three weeks of Harmac's closure, the employees made it known they were considering buying and operating the mill. "A lot of people were thinking that Harmac went broke. Harmac didn't. It was Pope & Talbot," said Harmac employee-owner Rohn Brown in a 2008 CHEK news story about the mill. "We can make money at this mill. We can make this work, and I don't care what anybody says or anybody thinks. We're going to go back in there, and we're going to make money—for us."

It took three months, including two months of court proceedings, but on August 29, 2008, a group of Harmac employees, along with three private investors, put their money where their mouths were and took ownership of the mill. Each employee contributed $25,000 to the $13.2 million purchase price, giving the group a 25 per cent equity share in the Harmac Pulp Mill, now called Harmac Pacific.

Five weeks later, the mill reopened with a single production line and 210 employees. Since then, Harmac Pacific has restarted a second production line and significantly upgraded its facilities. The workforce now stands at about three hundred employees, each of whom is an employee-owner. Pulp production—at 365,000 to 380,000 tonnes a year—is almost back to the mill's pre-closure output.

"We've made the mill more efficient, so that has allowed us to increase our tonnage," said Harmac president Levi Sampson. "But we don't have any plans at this point [for] growing the mill any further than our two-line operation." More than half the pulp produced at Harmac is sold into China, he said, with another 20 per cent going to Japan, Korea, and Australia. "We're in the top [sales] percentile for sure within Canada."

Today, Harmac Pacific is jointly owned by the employee group and two private investors: the Vancouver-based Sampson Group and Pioneer Log Homes, of Williams Lake, BC. The third organization in the original partnership group, construction company Totzauer Holdings, is no longer with Harmac.

Levi Sampson, who led his family's involvement with the mill, is a keen proponent of the employee-ownership model. "This is the most motivated workforce I've ever seen," he said in the *Nanaimo Daily News* in 2008, at the time of the mill purchase. "[The employees] are willing to weather the bad times when the markets are down, but will have happy days when the markets are good."

Six years later, Sampson is even more convinced that the employee-ownership model is a good one. The workers are invested financially and emotionally, he said, meaning nobody ever refuses to go above and beyond the tasks laid out in a job description. "Now everybody will do anything they are qualified for and capable of doing. If something needs to be done and, for example, someone has to work through lunch, it's not even a case of a supervisor has to ask them to do that. They'll just be happy to go ahead and get that done. Or if someone needs to stay after work to make something happen, it's just done."

Another benefit of the employee-ownership model defies explanation. "Our sick days and injury days are a fraction of what they were in the past. For whatever reason, that changes when you have ownership in the company," said Sampson, adding that, in 2008, the unionized Harmac employees also signed an "unprecedented" eleven-year labour agreement, giving the company stability until at least 2019. That means customers are guaranteed their pulp supplies won't be interrupted by work stoppages or lockouts, something that gives Harmac an added advantage.

While other mills have closed their doors and laid off staff in the wake of reduced demand and falling prices, "the Harmac pulp mill continues to be a bright light of success," wrote reporter Robert Barron in the *Nanaimo Daily News* in spring 2012.

To further buffer the business from the ups and downs of the pulp market, Harmac Pacific expanded its operations in a new direction in August 2013. Timed to coincide with its fifth anniversary as an employee-owned entity, Harmac built a $45 million power plant, fuelled by wood waste. The plant generates more than enough electricity to power Harmac's operations, and BC Hydro has agreed to buy the excess electricity—enough to power seventeen thousand homes annually—for at least fifteen years. "That's really important for our company, because the pulp market is so cyclical with these wild ups and downs," said Sampson. "Now we have this [other] steady stream. It makes it a lot easier to run the business and look forward to the future."

Remaining flush during a downturn in the industry and having enough cash to finance the power plant and other upgrades are indicators of the success of the employee-owned Harmac.

Sampson's explanation for this success? "We have one of the best, if not the best, cost structures in the pulp industry at Harmac thanks to our ownership model."

That model allows the company to be "lean and mean," he said. "We don't have a big corporate office. It's just the guys at the mill, and we handle all our marketing in-house. It means we get out there and visit our customers face to face. It's a different environment."

And it's an environment others are watching. Sampson is often called upon to talk to other company owners in a variety of industries about the benefits of the employee-ownership model.

The 2008 evolution of Harmac was a news story CHEK followed closely, producing more than twenty-six news pieces on the mill's closure and subsequent purchase by its employees. "That [story] really resonated with me," said Rob Germain, who now cites "the Harmac example," along with the bid by the CHCH employees in Hamilton, as "the inspiration" for the CHEK employees to purchase their workplace. "If it hadn't been for that, I doubt if any of this would have happened."

TO UNDERSTAND THE INNER workings of the Harmac purchase-by-employees, Germain contacted Levi Sampson the day after he and Pollard met with potential investors Harris and O'Connor. Sampson immediately agreed to serve as an adviser to the CHEK employee group—and perhaps take on an even more significant role. Minutes after he and Germain ended their first telephone call, Sampson "phoned right back" and said he would like to take a look at CHEK's business plan, said Germain. "So here's a guy who has a track record of pulling this off, and he's willing to be a consultant for us—and he may be interested in investing."

Over the following week, Sampson met with CHEK staff and management, toured the station, liaised with Tom Harris in Nanaimo, and reviewed the business plan. "It looked pretty sound," said Sampson. "I definitely combed through everything, seeing if this was feasible to do, and how much the employees would have to come to the table with to make it a real, genuinely employee-owned model where they had a stake in the company."

What really impressed him, though, was the determination of the CHEK staff. "There was a real sense of 'We can do this. We'll do anything to make this work.' That's what you need—and until I see that, I wouldn't ever want to make an investment, because in an employee-owned model, you're only as good as your people."

On July 28, just six days after Canwest issued layoff notices, CHEK management, heartened by the interest of Sampson and the other financiers, hosted its first formal all-staff meeting, an "exploratory meeting . . . to discuss possible employee ownership," said Germain. They talked about the Harmac story, possible investors, the value of CHEK's newscasts to advertisers, and the urgency with which a deal would have to be made if the employees chose to move forward with a bid. "There was a lot of enthusiasm [at the meeting]. We weren't asking anybody to sign up at that point. We were just saying it's possible—and here's why. It was enough of a positive reaction that we were able to keep going . . . and report back to the investors as well that we had some positive feedback."

That meeting generated the first media story on the subject. On July 30, the *Nanaimo Daily News* reported on a possible "Harmac-style employee takeover of Victoria-based CHEK television," with a caveat from Germain: "It's premature to say too much about that now."

While CHEK managers certainly knew how to operate a television station, they didn't necessarily know how to go about buying one—so they started asking questions. While general manager John Pollard approached the CRTC, news director Rob Germain further investigated Harmac's formula for success and researched financial incentives available to CHEK. Meanwhile, assignment editor and union president Richard Konwick focused on the possibility of employee purchase from a union perspective.

So much was happening so quickly and simultaneously at this point that it's virtually impossible to document the activities in any kind of chronological order. Instead, I will summarize the processes that took place during the following weeks.

CRTC Requirements

One of the first people John Pollard contacted for information—even before the first all-staff meeting—was Stephen Simpson, the CRTC's regional commissioner for BC and Yukon. Simpson and Pollard had met a few months earlier at a BC broadcasters' conference. "Even at that time, John had intimated that they [CHEK] were not prepared to become roadkill as a byproduct of the consequences of Canwest's endeavours to try and right the ship or bankrupt the organization," said Simpson in the summer of 2012. "So I was aware of their intent way back."

In July, after Canwest confirmed its decision to close CHEK, Simpson said he and Pollard spoke again:

> John had very few places to go. They were going to be shuttered . . . So his first calls to me were really quite perfunctory. It was, "Hey, I just want to go on notice with somebody that we would like to stop this from happening. And that would obviously be through a negotiation to buy CHEK from the parent company. What's involved in terms of transferring licences? What happens?" He really didn't know.
>
> My job initially was really just to walk him through the stages of where our interests lay and the processes and hoops we would make him go through. That was to a large extent the

substance of the conversation. The rest of it would have to be taken up between him and his employees on one end, and that group and Canwest on the other—and those discussions [the CRTC] wouldn't be part of.

Later that summer, while Pollard was overseas on vacation, Germain continued the discussions with Simpson, who told him CHEK needed two things: "a memorandum of understanding" formalizing the CHEK group's intent to buy the station, which would trigger the CRTC to get involved, and an agreement between Canwest and CHEK that the station's new owners would assume responsibility for all operating costs during the transfer-of-licence process.

Simpson told Germain the CRTC would "expedite" the hearing process, but the licence transfer could still take four to six months, starting with a forty-five- to sixty-day period of public notice. That would give anyone who wanted to weigh in on the transaction a chance to do so. "Beyond that, there might be a September or October hearing, so it would be November [or] December before we got a decision," said Germain. During that time, Canwest, as the licence holder, would be responsible for station operations. "They were not going to stomach any losses during that time, so we [CHEK] would have to cover those losses."

At the time, CHEK had no advertising or programming booked beyond August 31, and salaries and operating expenses would have to be covered during the crossover period. "We did the math [to figure out] how much we needed to cover those costs," said Germain. Based on a "worst-case scenario [meaning zero revenue for the first four months], we came up with a figure of $2.5 million."

Tax Credits and Other Financial Incentives

Through Levi Sampson, Rob Germain connected with Harmac's lawyer to learn as much as he could about the pulp mill deal. During that discussion, he discovered the Harmac employees had been eligible for a 30 per cent investment tax credit—something that might also be applicable to CHEK employees if they chose to buy the station. For specifics, Germain contacted "the same guy at the provincial government ministry" who had helped the Harmac staff. Ultimately, the CHEK group took advantage of a different, but equally valuable, tax credit through the same program Harmac had used.

The Small Business Venture Capital Program was designed "to help small businesses in British Columbia access capital for business start-up and expansion." To take advantage of the tax credit, CHEK set up an Eligible Business Corporation (EBC) called CHEK Media Group. The Investment Capital Program Guidelines laid out the rules and returns of the tax credit:

> Investments in an EBC are made without guarantee of return and must be held for at least five years . . .
>
> Individuals who purchase shares of an EBC are eligible to receive a refundable tax credit equal to 30% of their investment amount, up to a maximum of $60,000 in credits per taxation year. Corporations may only deduct the tax credit from British Columbia taxes otherwise payable under the Income Tax Act (British Columbia). . . .
>
> Excess tax credits, either corporate or personal, may be carried forward and used in any of the four subsequent taxation years.

To qualify for the program, EBCs must "be substantially engaged in British Columbia" in one of five "qualifying activities." The CHEK Media Group qualified under "development of interactive digital new media product," defined in the literature as a product that "educates, informs or entertains and presents information using at least two of the mediums of text, sound or visual images."

Germain forwarded this new information to potential investors via email. "Even though CHEK is old media, it's eligible because it will soon be transmitting digitally, as well as developing interactive content online," he wrote.

What this tax credit meant to everyone, including employees, who bought shares in the newly formed CHEK Media Group was that they would get almost one-third of their investment dollars back come income tax time. Learning about this program "was a major development," said Germain, "because if you're sitting on the fence trying to decide whether or not this is a good investment, suddenly this makes it a pretty good investment, or at least a lot more attractive." In addition, for individuals, money invested in the CHEK Media Group would qualify as an RRSP contribution, meaning it would reduce their taxable income.

Meanwhile, early in July 2009, the CRTC had announced details of its new Local Programming Improvement Fund (LPIF), which was to begin offering financing to small- and mid-market television stations in September 2009. Under the fund, the CHEK group calculated it would be eligible for $2.3 million a year, further boosting the financial viability of purchasing the station.

Bringing Investors On Board

On August 4, two weeks after she'd issued layoff notices, Canwest senior vice-president Chris McGinley told Germain that Canwest would entertain "one last offer" for CHEK. That meant employees and investors would have to move quickly if they were to put together a bid.

On August 5, CHEK management hosted interested investors Michael O'Connor, Levi Sampson, and Tom Harris, along with a group of executives and family members from the Tom Harris Group, a Nanaimo-based business that included Tom Harris Cellular and a collection of car dealerships called the Harris Auto Group. Germain has dubbed this meeting with investors "The Dragon's Den." Like the CBC-TV show of the same name, this Dragon's Den was a venue for budding entrepreneurs (in this case, the CHEK group) to make a pitch to convince the "dragons" (investors) to back their business idea.

Representing CHEK were Germain, Bill Pollock, and John Pollard, who attended via speakerphone from Scotland where he was officially on vacation but continued participating in CHEK discussions via telephone, email, text, and Skype. "It was a stressful meeting and . . . not everybody from the Tom Harris group left convinced," said Germain. Tom's son Tony, general manager of Harris Mitsubishi in Nanaimo, "was the most bullish, wanting to go ahead with this. [He and Tom] said they were interested enough that they wanted to meet with the rest of the [CHEK] staff and get a sense of where we were going."

Immediately after the "Dragon's Den" meeting, Germain sent an email to all CHEK staff:

I want to inform you about the outcome of a meeting today with a group of potential investors. The investors came to CHEK, toured the facility and met for four hours with Bill, John (who was on speakerphone) and me. The discussions went well. The majority of investors indicated they wanted to proceed to the next step, which includes meeting with staff. Because of the urgency, we agreed to set the meeting for this Friday at noon.

At the meeting, you will hear from Levi Sampson, President of Harmac Pacific, who will share the experience at Harmac and explain how employee ownership has been key to turning the money-losing operation in Nanaimo into a profitable one in the first year. We will also be discussing CHEK's proposed business plan that we believe can return this company to profitability and local ownership. The investors in attendance will be gauging the level of interest by staff to make that happen. We will also be discussing the financial investment that will be asked of employees. But this is just an information meeting. There will be no formal vote at this time.

By the time the meeting took place, the executives from Tom Harris Cellular had "decided to take a pass," said Germain. But Tony Harris, along with O'Connor and Sampson, met with CHEK management and staff on Friday, August 7.

Encouraging Staff

While efforts to recruit major investors were underway, so were efforts to satisfy staff that buying the station was a sound idea. Since the first staff meeting (July 28), Germain and Pollock had been "talking one-on-one to staff, trying to get them onside," wrote Germain in an email to the vacationing John Pollard. "Hopefully, we can make the employee purchase as painless as possible."

At the August 7 staff-and-investors meeting, Germain and Pollock introduced the players and reviewed a proposed model for employee ownership. Employees were not yet asked to make a decision about participating in the purchase of the station, but the next day, the story was out that they were considering it. The *Times Colonist* reported:

CHEK-TV employees met with community members yesterday to discuss ways to stave off the planned closing of the television station at month's end.

"We have high hopes that we can pull this off," said news director Rob Germain. The noon meeting examined an employee-ownership business plan for the station that would see local content boosted, he said. "We are seeking expertise from the community for this plan." . . .

CHEK staff hope to keep B.C.'s oldest television station on the air by becoming owners, with outside investors participating as well. Germain would not reveal names of potential investors . . .

Employees are the driving force behind the plan and are in the process of making decisions, he said.

The same day this article appeared in the newspaper, CHEK produced its own news story announcing a possible employee purchase. The following day, August 9, a second CHEK news story featured three Victoria-area politicians voicing their support for the employees' efforts to save CHEK. Rob Germain was also interviewed for the news piece. As a tag to the story, news anchor Tess van Straaten asked viewers to email Canwest CEO Leonard Asper and call Canwest head office to voice their support for saving the station. She provided all the necessary contact information.

The next day, Germain heard from Global BC vice-president and general manager Brett Manlove. "[Canwest] didn't appreciate getting the phone calls and the emails," said Germain. "[Manlove] said, 'You're still working for the company, and the company has a spokesperson, and that's John Douglas. So refer all requests to head office, and we'll deal with it there.'"

Germain sent a note to news staff reminding them to be objective in their reporting of the situation.

Union Assistance

By this time, having had two meetings about possible employee ownership of CHEK, staff knew that Levi Sampson's participation as an investor was conditional on the employees also buying shares in the station. "It would show that [they] were serious, not only to myself, but to other potential investors," said Sampson.

For the CHEK group to raise enough money to satisfy Sampson, each full-time staffer was asked to kick in $15,000, with part-timers contributing $7,500 to the purchase of the station. (Management contributions were higher.)

Understandably, not everyone at CHEK had $15,000 on hand to invest. With that in mind, Richard Konwick, president of the Victoria unit of the Communications, Energy and Paperworkers Union (CEP), approached Mark Cameron, then president of the larger Canwest union local to ask for help. "I said, 'Can we get any money? Can we [the union] do anything?'"

For Vancouver-based Cameron, the immediate answer was yes, the union would help. "It was the right thing to do," he said. "It was about protecting our members and protecting their jobs." After consulting with board members, Cameron confirmed that the union would, in fact, offer financial support to CHEK employees.

A year earlier, this would not have been possible, said Konwick, who has been CHEK's union president since 2006. To understand why the union was now able to assist financially, "you have to go back to the point where Canwest bought the television assets of WIC, which included CHEK," he said.

At the time, BCTV and CHEK had been considered a single unit when it came to negotiating union contracts. Otherwise, each Global and WIC station had bargained under a separate CEP local with a separate union contract—meaning that, when Canwest bought WIC, it made for a cumbersome system for union and management.

"The heads of the locals at the Global stations and the heads of the locals at the WIC stations . . . got together and said, instead of thirteen separate contracts, we should have one contract for the whole company," said Konwick. "Instead of having separate stations, separate contracts, [we should] have one employer, one contract."

The process to unite all the locals under a single certification involved the Canadian Industrial Relations Board (CIRB) and "dragged on for years and years and years and years, from roughly the early 2000s until 2008, when it became pretty apparent that Canwest was in serious trouble," said Konwick. At that point, individual union leaders decided to abandon their efforts to create a single unit with a single contract—they needed to do something that would allow them to band together more quickly. The rationale, he said, was as follows:

> We have no idea what's going to happen, but there is a pretty good chance that some very bad things are going to happen. We decided that it would be better to have some survivors looking after the ones who didn't survive.
>
> In the spring of 2009, we voted to merge all our separate locals into one big local. So all the Canwest stations became one local. What that allowed was a pooling of money, which [would become] critical [for CHEK] in a couple of months. Of course, we didn't know it then.

Even though the smaller locals had merged into one big coalition, each station continued to maintain its own union "unit." Under this new structure, Canwest no longer had thirteen locals with thirteen contracts. Instead, it had one local with thirteen contracts. It was this larger local—called CEP Media One (M1)—that Konwick contacted in August 2009 when the staff in the Victoria unit needed help coming up with cash to buy shares in CHEK.

M1 was willing—and now able—to pitch in. "They gave everybody an interest-free $3,500 loan (for full-time employees), which basically covered half the initial payment," said Konwick. "The payment was broken into two [installments]—the first one, $7,500, was due immediately, and six months later, the other $7,500 was due. So 50 per cent of that [first payment] was covered, so people only had to come up with another $4,000, which is a lot easier on very, very, very short notice to do."

For then-M1 president Cameron, what Canwest was doing "was unjust, and it was wrong, and it's so rare that you actually have a chance [to] go in and fix the world and make it a little better place. That was sort of the motivation for helping."

Individual CEP units from the Global stations in Calgary, Edmonton, and Vancouver would later offer further support, each contributing another $15,000 to the CHEK cause.

ARMED WITH FINANCIAL BACKING from the union, along with information about the LPIF and tax incentives, having lobbied serious investors and knowing what the CRTC required, CHEK management called another all-staff meeting. On August 10, Germain and Pollock, in person, and Pollard, on the phone from Scotland, ran staff through the details of the plan to buy the station—revenue and cost projections, programming options, financial opportunities, CRTC needs. This time, though, they asked staff to make a commitment. "We gave them until the next day at noon to make their declaration whether they were in or out," said Germain.

For reporter Veronica Cooper, the decision was easy:

> Having spent more than half my life working at CHEK (I was hired at twenty-two years old), I am so proud of what we do here every day. I really believe in this station—the importance of having a local voice, of telling stories about Islanders that otherwise might not get told . . . It was a leap of faith for each of us to invest our own savings . . . yet I couldn't stand by and let CHEK fade to black without trying to save it. And having watched Harmac employees bring their mill back from the brink was an inspiring goal to emulate!

Sales rep Howard Harding was equally sold on the idea. "I thought it was a terrific opportunity," he said in the summer of 2012. "I never thought I'd have a chance to buy a TV station in my life. I thought I'd jump in with both feet and give it a go. There was no question in my mind—I thought we could really make a go of it." Harding and his wife, Crystal, were both CHEK employees, and both opted in, as did most of the staff.

But not all employees were convinced buying the station was a good idea. One person was particularly vocal in his apprehension about the idea. "He wasn't saying don't do this," said Germain. "He was saying, 'You know, you have other options . . .' I was out there just doing my best sales job possible. I was standing before the group, and then he comes up and says, 'You know you can get a lot of retraining under EI.' . . . I was upset that he was going to derail the whole thing, and I was surprised that he was so ready to throw in the towel."

In the end, that particular staffer wasn't the only one to opt out. A total of seven employees—two editors, two cameramen, an engineer, a receptionist, and a reporter/anchor—chose to leave. But not all of them opted out because they thought the employee purchase was a bad idea. One employee was ready to retire, another had already planned to move out of province around that time, and a third was building a new house, meaning his priorities had changed. One of the seven actually opted back in six months later and continues to work at CHEK today.

Still, all departing employees benefitted from a union requirement that they get severance pay. "That became very controversial," said Konwick, explaining that all workers who chose to move on received regular paycheques for six to twelve months after taking their leave from the station. "It became a financial liability for CHEK."

One person who might have chosen to retire at the time but didn't was reporter Bruce Kirkpatrick, who had worked at CHEK for almost thirty-seven years at that point. He explained his decision to stay:

> I had heard via the grapevine that more people were taking the buyout than expected, and that was really hurting the station financially. So I saved them about $80,000 by not retiring, because they would have had to replace me [and pay a second salary]. The personal reason is that I wasn't ready to give it up. I thought, "OK, fine, so you get a year's salary. Then what? And what are you going to do in that year you've got the salary?" . . . So I made the decision to be part of the change.

By noon on August 11, the deadline to pledge their support, a total of thirty-three full- and part-time employees had signed on to buy the station. Germain and Konwick called the media to share the news. And Global BC vice-president Brett Manlove arrived in Victoria "to keep us from going rogue," said Germain.

Less than three weeks had passed since Canwest had announced it was closing CHEK—and less than three weeks remained before the station was scheduled to fade to black.

An early look at the CHEK control room and sets. When CHEK launched in 1956, it was the first station to take to the airwaves on Vancouver Island and the first independently owned station in British Columbia. COURTESY OF CHEK

Ida Clarkson (*third from right*), "Victoria's First Lady of Television," began her career as a copywriter but quickly proved her natural talent as an on-air personality. Clarkson was the popular host of a daily talk show on CHEK that aired for thirty years. COURTESY OF CHEK

CHEK's first locally produced show was *TV House Party*, hosted by longtime radio deejay Norm Pringle *(below, left)*. It was on this show that sixteen-year-old Jim Smith *(below, right)*, made his debut. Smith is credited with being the world's first Elvis impersonator. COURTESY OF GARRY PRINGLE

Barton & Co., a one-hour daily talk show hosted by veteran broadcaster John Barton, ran for six years (1976–82) on CHEK. It was groundbreaking in its own way, said the show's host three decades later. One of Barton's more memorable guests was Betty White, who ended up making an R-rated comment on live TV!
COURTESY OF CHEK

Three decades of TV cameras bearing three different CHEK logos, reflecting changing times and changing station ownership from the 1970s *(top)*, '80s *(middle)*, and '90s *(bottom)*. The middle photo shows Brian Mulroney on a 1988 visit to Victoria, being interviewed by CHEK's Jane Wilson, then-host of *Daily Edition*. The 1990s-era photo shows CHEK reporter Howard Markson. COURTESY OF CHEK

Student Forum was hosted in the 1970s by Marlene Palmer. COURTESY OF CHEK

Shake-It-Up, a dance show for teenagers in the mid-'80s, was hosted by Kristin Eriksen *(shown holding microphone)*. COURTESY OF CHEK

Capital Comment was a weekly political affairs show where politicians and members of the BC Legislative Press Gallery came together to discuss the issues of the day. This episode featured Jim Hume (*left*) and Vaughn Palmer (*centre*). CHEK's Andy Stephen (not shown) hosted the program for twenty years. COURTESY OF CHEK

CHEK on-air personalities Robin Adair and Marisa Antinucci met on the job and were married in 1987. COURTESY OF CHEK

This photo of the CHEK on-air team was taken in September 1984, just after the station's headquarters moved to its current location on Kings Road. *Left to right:* Harry Maunu, Patty Pitts, Susan Long, Bruce Kirkpatrick *(sitting)*, Mike Farquhar, Tony Cox, Robin Adair, Mark Jan Vrem *(sitting)*, Marisa Antinucci, Bill Pollock, and Alex Robertson. COURTESY OF CHEK

A photo of the on-air news team from the early 2000s, when CHEK was part of the Canwest Global empire and rebranded as CH. Back *(left to right)*: Ed Bain, Hudson Mack, Meribeth Burton, and Vee Cooper; front row *(seated)*: Stacy Ross and Gordie Tupper. COURTESY OF CHEK

This picture, taken on August 31, 2009, shows an electronic billboard outside Victoria's sports arena flashing the *Times Colonist*'s headline of the day: "CHEK TV could fade to black tonight." The photo is now framed on news director Rob Germain's office wall, a reminder of how far CHEK has come since that day, when no one was sure whether the station would survive. COURTESY OF CHEK

six

CLOSING THE DEAL

It may be too late to save the latest local station to be put under the axe in what Canadian networks have decried as a "broken" broadcasting model.

—**James Keller,** Canadian Press, August 13, 2009

THE DAY CHEK EMPLOYEES pledged to buy the station, Global BC vice-president Brett Manlove set up a temporary office at CHEK. He met in person with news director Rob Germain and via telephone with general manager John Pollard, who was still on vacation in Scotland. Manlove laid out the conditions the CHEK employees would have to meet for Canwest to consider entering negotiations. They would have to submit an official letter of intent, prove they had enough funds to carry CHEK through the transfer-of-ownership period, and provide details about private investors.

The day Manlove arrived in Victoria, Canwest also assigned Andrew Akman, senior vice-president of strategic and business development, as the "point person" for CHEK negotiations. A former vice-president at Alliance Atlantis, Akman had joined Canwest when the two companies merged their executive offices in 2008.

Over the next three days, newspapers from Port Alberni, BC, to Saint John, NB, covered the CHEK story, most using files from this article in the *Times Colonist*:

CHEK-TV employees have committed more than $500,000 in a bid to create an employee-owned company to save the station. The plan would see staff have 25 per cent ownership, with the balance held by outside investors, news director Rob Germain said yesterday. "Employees have overwhelmingly come forward to put up funds," Germain said . . .

Employees met Monday evening and had until noon yesterday [August 11] to deliver a signed pledge. The goal of $500,000 was surpassed, Germain said. "It is obviously an exciting time and today was a significant day, I hope, in the history of CHEK News." . . .

Germain said the aim is to get a letter of intent to Canwest Global within the next 24 hours. Significant steps still remain. An offer has to be made and accepted by the company. "They are holding the door open for us and we appreciate that greatly."

On August 12, Victoria's CBC Radio aired a lengthy, live, in-studio segment with Germain and union president Richard Konwick about the possibility of an employee purchase. Later that day, Manlove forbid further interviews by members of CHEK management. Manlove was in a tough position, noted Germain, because privately, he supported the CHEK group, but his job dictated that he enforce Canwest's position. Still, at that point, Konwick became the sole spokesperson for the CHEK employees. "Rob and John were told they'd be out the door, essentially, if they said anything," said Konwick. "So, speaking for the union, I became the person who did the interviews and did a lot of getting our message out. I represented something. I could speak on behalf of [the union]."

It is interesting to note that, while Manlove was working with CHEK staff in Victoria, and a week earlier Canwest vice-president Chris McGinley had told CHEK management the company would entertain "one last offer" for the station, Canwest spokesperson John Douglas continued to insist there was nothing in the works. "The company hasn't seen a proposal from the CHEK employees—or even been told one is coming," he said, as quoted in a Canadian Press article the same day Germain and Konwick did their CBC interview.

As the August 31 deadline loomed, the CHEK group became more and more frustrated with Canwest's "lies" and "negativity," said Germain. "Every time they were asked about [the employee purchase proposal] by any other media, they were constantly saying, 'We don't know anything about this. We haven't heard from these guys. We don't know if they're serious.' And we're going, 'How can they say that? We're talking to them all the time.' Publicly, they were trying to make us look as lost as they could."

Privately, Canwest would not even enter a discussion with the CHEK team. "Boy, they were buggers to work with," said operations manager Bill Pollock. "They were in shut-down mode, and they just did not want to talk about selling the station or anything. As far as they were concerned, it was done. It really took a huge effort to turn them around to start to listen to us."

Knowing they couldn't do this alone, the CHEK employees turned to the public to help forward the cause. In February, immediately after Canwest said it would either sell CHEK or shut it down, host/producer Dana Hutchings started a "Save CHEK News" page on Facebook. Within a week, the page had more than 2,000 members. By July 22, the day Canwest announced its decision to close CHEK, the Facebook membership had grown modestly, to about 2,800. Within three weeks of that announcement, though, membership skyrocketed to more than 8,600 fans, said Hutchings.

The support "was shocking, absolutely stunning," she said. And it motivated CHEK staff to keep going in their bid to purchase the station. "We had that instant affirmation that, yes, there will be support for us if we go ahead and try. [That] motivation was huge for us in terms of getting to our goal. Without it, I don't think we could have gotten through it."

Hutchings read Facebook posts every day. "Having [people] say, 'we love you,' or 'here's how you've inspired us,' or 'here's why we need you in the community'" helped her maintain a positive outlook during that exhausting, emotional summer. Not every comment on the Facebook page was friendly, though. "There was a lot of negative input about Canwest," she said, "but we tried with the site to keep it really positive. I was deleting comments every day about 'bleeping, bleeping Canwest.'"

The site did such a good job of conveying the Save CHEK News message that, in mid-August, Canwest told CHEK to shut down the Facebook page. Hutchings refused. "It did put pressure on them," she said. "People would phone and go on the [Facebook] page and say, 'What can we do?' And I had no problem giving them the phone number to call Canwest and put some pressure on. I know they were inundated with calls, and that's when they tried to shut down the Facebook page. They said, 'You can't do that. It's a conflict with your job.' And [I said], 'Really? You gave me a pink slip.'"

Instead, Hutchings launched a Twitter account, adding another forum to convey the Save CHEK News message. "I give social media huge, huge credit for the role they played in getting the message out," she said. "It was really interesting how social media, new media, helped traditional media in this case."

In addition to showing allegiance on Facebook and Twitter, fans of the station phoned with words of encouragement or to offer money (which CHEK did not accept), and they wrote letters to Canwest and the CRTC on CHEK's behalf. One Victoria resident wore his support for the station on his sleeve—literally.

The day Canwest announced its decision to close CHEK, Bill Wellbourn started a Save CHEK News T-shirt campaign. Born and raised in Victoria, Wellbourn had been "watching CHEK forever," and refused to let the fifty-three-year-old station go down without a fight. He wanted to make sure "people understood that if we lose the channel, it's gone forever."

At the time, Wellbourn worked as a sales rep for Ocean Promotion, a company that brands sportswear and other promotional items. Through his work, he had dealt with CHEK on many occasions, and had become friends with the station's general manager, John Pollard. "I knew these guys pretty well, and I grew up watching them. It was that simple."

Wellbourn's original goal was to sell a few dozen "Save CHEK News" T-shirts through stores and businesses on Vancouver Island to raise "street-level awareness" about the plight of CHEK and to raise money for a local charity. His charity of choice was Jeneece Place, founded by Victoria teen Jeneece Edroff as a home away from home for families of children who travel to Victoria for medical care.

"I thought if we sold one hundred T-shirts, that would be so cool, and we'd get one hundred people talking about this," said Wellbourn.

In the end, he and his colleagues sold 1,446 shirts and donated more than $7,500 to Jeneece Place. "It snowballed into this thing where people were volunteering to help me distribute shirts," said Wellbourn. "It was crazy. It was really cool. It was addictive seeing so many people into saving the station."

Requests for T-shirts came from as far away as New Brunswick and Yukon. Local police officers and the mayor of Victoria posed for photos wearing Save CHEK News T-shirts. Former CHEK employees phoned to request shirts. Other fans of the station posted YouTube videos of themselves wearing the T-shirts at concerts and public events. "It was this momentum that went crazy," said Wellbourn. "It wasn't like a grand business plan. It was more street level. It was local people taking care of local people."

As an aside, after the employees bought the station, about four hundred Save CHEK News T-shirts remained, unsold, in stores. "We requested all the shirts to come back to our shop and I [printed] a D on them and put them back out there," said Wellbourn. The new *Saved* CHEK News T-shirts sold out in a few days. "It was a good way to wrap it up."

Dana Hutchings calls the T-shirt campaign "the big one" in terms of community initiatives to save the station. "It was a huge visual reminder."

Rob Germain agrees the "outpouring of support from the community" was crucial to saving the station, but he points out that gathering this support was a little more strategic than it may have appeared:

We work in the news business. We know what it takes to [create] a campaign that resonates with the public. We strategized right from the beginning. We knew that, for us to be able to do anything, the public needed to believe that the station was going to be closed, and they needed to be outraged about that. It wasn't hard to do that because that was reality. We knew that that was something we could harness—that outrage in the public—and that it was something we could use to pressure

Canwest to do the right thing. They owned the *Times Colonist* and Global BC and the *Nanaimo Daily News* . . . They had a lot of properties in British Columbia, and they [wouldn't] want to have a black eye and be the bad guy. Obviously they wanted to appear to be the good corporate citizen. So we strategized and created a campaign to try to shame them into doing the right thing.

Germain said the CHEK group "strategically" released "bits of information" on Facebook and to the media. For example, he and his colleagues let it be known they'd had an all-staff meeting to discuss the possibility of employee ownership, and they put out the word the day the employees pledged their money to buy the station.

"It was that strategy that in the end, I think, won the day," said Germain. "It didn't matter what the business plan was. It didn't matter what everything else was. If we didn't have that strategy to pressure Canwest, we would have been closed and gone."

It wasn't just members of the public who lobbied Canwest to save CHEK. On August 13, then-MP Denise Savoie sent an email to Canwest CEO Leonard Asper, urging him "to consider selling Victoria's CHEK-TV to the coalition led by its employees," adding, "their viewers and the entire Greater Victoria community stand behind them, and I implore you to not deny them this opportunity to make it happen."

Company spokesperson John Douglas replied on Asper's behalf: "We understand that there are efforts at the community level to put an employee purchase plan together, but we have not yet seen a proposal nor do we have any assurance that one is coming." He continued, outlining "the significant hurdles that will be required to put together a last-minute bid," including preparing a business plan and programming schedule, getting CRTC approval, and covering projected operating losses. He wrote:

I wish it were as easy as simply moving a date to accommodate these efforts. However it is not. When we announced the review at the beginning of February, we said that we would not continue to operate the station beyond August 31. We announced in June that we have not purchased a programming schedule for the stations, including CHEK, beyond August 31. When we announced that we were closing the station, we stopped selling any advertising beyond the closure date. In other words, there is no programming or advertising to support an operation after August 31.

Within days of Savoie lending her voice to the campaign, Rob Germain contacted another local politician for help. After receiving "a 24th hour panic call," then-MP and Minister of State for Sports Gary Lunn agreed to meet with Germain, Levi Sampson, and John Pollard (who had by then returned from his vacation).

"They said, 'We have a plan where we can rescue the station, but we can't even get anybody at Canwest to take our calls,'" remembered Lunn. "'We are just locked out. Can you help us?'"

Lunn, who had met Leonard Asper on a number of occasions in the past, immediately cancelled all his appointments for the coming week, booked a meeting with Asper, and flew to Winnipeg to see him. Lunn explained his decision to get involved:

What motivated me to cancel my entire week and do this, the single biggest factor, was that the employees believed in themselves enough that they were prepared to put their own skin in the game. They were prepared to put their own money up, which spoke volumes. They weren't coming to the government saying, "Can you get me $10 million to save CHEK-TV? Can you get the government to buy it?" They weren't asking for a dime. They were saying, "Help us save our own TV station and our jobs. We believe in ourselves enough that we can make this work." So I at least had to make the effort to do everything I could to give them that shot.

UP TO THIS POINT, CHEK management had been trying to *talk* to Canwest, trying to reach a verbal agreement-in-principle before forcing the discussion with a formal letter of intent. With less than two weeks to the shut-down date, and because Canwest executives "kept being difficult about it," said Germain, "we finally said, 'OK, let's get the bloody letter of intent.'"

On August 18, John Pollard put CHEK's intentions in writing to Canwest. The letter was addressed to negotiator Andrew Akman and copied to Leonard Asper, among other Canwest executives:

> Dear Mr. Akman,
>
> We represent a group of Vancouver Island-based investors including the employees of CHEK-TV. This letter makes formal our intent to enter a binding agreement with Canwest to take over operations of CHEK Television. Our intent is to have an agreement in principle for the asset purchase reached by or near Aug. 31, 2009.
>
> This agreement would have us assume all obligations of the operation of CHEK-TV after Sept. 1, 2009, until such time as regulatory approval has been given and the transfer of the license [sic] is complete. . . .
>
> We have been assured by representatives of the CRTC the commission will assist and expedite the transfer of licence application process. A copy of our proposed programming schedule has already been submitted.
>
> We have very strong community support and have received encouragement from elected officials from all parties in BC and Ottawa. As a group we would ensure that Canwest receives full credit for its cooperation in reaching an amicable agreement that will help keep CHEK-TV on the air and its staff employed.

Unfortunately for CHEK, Canwest didn't take the letter seriously as an offer to buy the station, said Asper in a 2013 interview. "It wasn't structured in a way that bondholder types could just say yes. It was very loosely worded. It was just like a proposal handwritten in [layperson's] English, whereas they needed to send a 20-page legal document."

In addition, he said, by this time, with just two weeks to go before CHEK was to close its doors, he and his colleagues were "just really,

really tired." For the past nine months, they had been negotiating with bondholders to save Canwest. They had been subjected to threats of closure and last-minute reprieves over and over again. "So the idea of trying to work on another deal was too much," he said. "We were trying to raise money from new investors to try to buy out the bondholders. There was just so much going on that [when it came to CHEK], people said we just really can't be bothered. Let's just let it go. It's just too much. It's in the 'too-hard' basket."

That said, a few days later, when Asper met with Gary Lunn for the first time, he changed his position.

At their first meeting on August 21, Lunn outlined the situation at CHEK and what the employees were trying to do. "It was very cordial," said Lunn, who felt the CEO was "sympathetic," but he knew what Asper was up against at that time. "The whole Canwest media empire" was falling apart around him, said Lunn. "The best analogy is that we have a smouldering flame here [at CHEK], and he's got forest fires burning all around him on all fronts. You're not going to deal with the small little flame when you've got forest fires closing in on you."

Still, Lunn managed to sway the Canwest exec. "Gary really impressed upon me how much CHEK meant to Victoria and the Island in general," said Asper. After that first discussion, Asper decided to help the CHEK group, and he agreed to meet with Lunn a few more times over the next few days. "I just decided, let's get this done, let's just make it happen." By then, though, Asper wasn't the one calling the shots at Canwest; the bondholders were. "But Gary gave me a boost of confidence to at least give it a shot," he said.

Asper knew he was taking a risk within the reorganized Canwest structure by helping CHEK and getting others involved. "We weren't doing anything wrong. We were just contravening an order to get rid of [CHEK]"—or at least contravening an order to get the station off the books and letting the bondholders off the hook, financially.

There was still much work to come, but the meetings between Lunn and Asper were considered a turning point that "broke down some of the barriers," Germain said later. Canwest, at the highest level, was now listening. From Lunn's perspective, "what I was able to do was open the door . . . and push hard. [CHEK] couldn't have gotten through to present their case. That's where I came in. From my connections, I had the ability."

Meanwhile, after receiving the letter of intent from CHEK—but before Lunn sat down with Asper for the first time—Canwest negotiator Andrew Akman met with CHEK management via conference call to discuss the employees' intentions. By this time, the CHEK group had collected a total financial commitment of about $2.5 million from employees and private investors—enough to cover worst-case-scenario operating costs during the transfer-of-licence period. During the conference call, though, Akman said $2.5 million wasn't enough. He said Canwest required *twice* that amount to cover potential losses for the three- to four-month time frame.

"We're just lay people," said Germain. "We're not financiers, we're not MBAs, and we're scratching our heads saying, 'Why do you need so much money?'"

After a series of back-and-forth emails, Akman confirmed, in writing, that Canwest would require a two-part, partially non-refundable deposit of $5 million. "Deposit is composed of Part A ($2.5M related to Canwest's structural and fixed costs associated with keeping the station open beyond August 31st) and Part B ($2.5M related to estimated operating losses between Sep 1 and Dec 31)." He then described a complicated formula by which Canwest would determine how much of the deposit money CHEK would forfeit under various circumstances.

At that point, Akman suggested the CHEK team hire an experienced lawyer, something Leonard Asper also recognized the group needed. Without proper legal counsel, Asper said, he knew the bondholders would never take CHEK's offer seriously.

"The key to me," he remembered, "was finding someone who could represent the employee group, who could write the deal out and negotiate the deal in such a way that the bondholders would accept it." With that in mind, he sent the word through the grapevine that CHEK might want to contact his friend and former law school classmate John Sandrelli, a Vancouver-based business lawyer. "I knew he was a restructuring lawyer," said Asper. "He was one of those lawyers who often represents companies in distress, or bondholders that are trying to force companies into distress. So he knew the type of people we were dealing with."

On August 21, CHEK retained Sandrelli. "He and Asper were buddies," said John Pollard, "and if you look back, that is probably one of the reasons the deal got done." What Sandrelli was able to do, added Rob Germain, was "get around Andrew Akman" and become "a pipeline to Asper."

To engage Sandrelli, though, CHEK needed to come up with a $20,000 retainer, money the group didn't have. Once again, the union stepped in—and this time, it was CHEK's own CEP unit that came to the rescue. "By chance, over the years, our local here had run a little surplus every year, and there was about $20,000 sitting in the account," said Richard Konwick. "So I said, 'OK, the union will pay the deposit.' So the very, very first money, cash, that went into saving CHEK was union money."

Retainer paid, and with the August 31 deadline just ten days away, Sandrelli and his colleague Gary Sollis started working on CHEK's case.

After an introductory conference call with Akman and the CHEK group, Sandrelli called the $5 million deposit "absurd." At no point did Canwest offer an explanation for the seemingly inflated deposit requirement. "They said, 'We can't tell you,'" said Pollard, who offered to sign a non-disclosure agreement so that someone could explain it to him. Canwest refused to allow that.

"We just couldn't get it," said Germain. "What I think they did was, they found out how much we were planning on raising and they doubled it. I truly believe that's what they did. 'OK, you're planning on raising $2.5 million? We want five.' And they stuck to that right to the bitter end."

That's not exactly what happened, said Leonard Asper, who later acknowledged that $5 million had been excessive, and had been based on incorrect assumptions about CHEK's capacity to run the station, the CRTC's willingness to expedite the transfer-of-ownership process, and the abilities of all parties to negotiate a solution.

At the time, though, $5 million was the figure Canwest had calculated would be needed to cover potential operating losses during the transfer-of-licence period, along with any liabilities—severance packages, for example—that would come Canwest's way if the CRTC did *not* approve the sale. During the late-August negotiations with CHEK, Asper, who was by now holding private conversations with Sandrelli, suggested to Canwest executives that the $5 million deposit be reduced to $2.5 million. After several days' debate on the subject, his suggestion was dismissed.

AT THIS POINT, JUST one month had passed since Canwest had announced its intention to close CHEK. That month, and the following week, was later described by various staff members as "an emotional roller coaster," "a very intense emotional experience," and a "nervous but exciting" time. For Bill Pollock, who was part of the team negotiating with Canwest, it was nerve-wracking. "There were moments when we thought this just wasn't going to fly, that this just wasn't going to work." One of the hardest things through it all, he said, was the responsibility he felt to his co-workers:

> There was a core group, four of us who were working on it. We told everyone else, "Concentrate on your job. Just come in and do your job, and that will take your mind off it. Let us worry about the other stuff. We'll give it the best shot we can." . . .
>
> So people didn't show it, but you could tell they were pretty nervous. I was as nervous as anybody else. John and Rob and myself and Rod Munro our accountant, we were talking, literally, 24 hours a day and making phone calls, talking to anyone who would listen, trying to work out plans, how much it would cost to do this, that, and the next thing. And where were we going to get all this equipment [if CHEK stayed open]? . . . We were trying to keep ourselves busy and not worry.

In addition to the "core group" was a larger working group—including Dana Hutchings, Richard Konwick, and human resources manager Peggy Heyer—liaising with staff and the union, bringing ideas forward, and getting the community on board. "We worked every single day, [including] weekends and nights," said Hutchings.

In the final few days of August 2009, the pace further intensified. "It was about as tense a negotiation to purchase this place as it could be," said Pollard. "It was crazy. It was the most fun I've ever had really, but it was absolute insanity. We'd have two telephone conversations going at the same time . . . It was just like in the movies. It was crazy."

What the CHEK group didn't know was that things were just as crazy on the Canwest side, with more than a dozen Canwest executives and lawyers working on the CHEK proposal. During the last week of August, they sent almost one hundred internal emails back and forth, addressing everything from how to word a response letter to CHEK to the CRTC approval process involved in a transfer-of-ownership to the potential financial liabilities for Canwest and its bondholders if the CHEK group bought the station. They held in-person and telephone meetings. Andrew Akman even returned from his vacation to continue negotiations with CHEK. And unbeknownst to the rest of the players, Asper and CHEK's lawyer Sandrelli shared many off-the-record phone calls during the latter part of August, working together behind the scenes on the CHEK deal.

"Basically, people worked seven, eight, nine days in a row, around the clock, in that late-August period and early September period to get the deal done," said Asper.

From CHEK's perspective, though, Canwest "negotiated hard and negotiated nasty," said John Pollard. Following is a portion of an email dialogue, dated Wednesday, August 26, between Canwest negotiator Akman and CHEK lawyer Sandrelli that illustrates Pollard's assessment.

The subject of discussion was finalizing an Asset Purchase Agreement (APA), a document setting out the terms of the sale of the station from Canwest to the CHEK Media Group, including assets to be transferred, costs, and timelines.

FROM: Sandrelli, John
SENT: Wednesday August 26, 2009 7:29 p.m.

Andrew,
        You will be receiving the APA and the Escrow Agreement tonight. I confirm that we do now have $1 million on deposit

so far that we are holding in escrow. I trust that is sufficient to at least get on a call tomorrow so Gary [Sollis] and I can take you through the major items. You do not necessarily have to review tonight but a call will be helpful.

FROM: Akman, Andrew
SENT: Wednesday, August 26, 2009 8:15 p.m.

John, when we speak I'd like you to walk me through how you see us getting to the "finish line" given the following outstanding issues:

- we require a binding offer to respond to, not a draft APA

- we require funds in escrow in the full amount discussed to keep the station open beyond Aug 31

- now that we better understand your client's requirements we have done detailed reviews of the cost of programming, master control, program scheduling, promo scheduling, and traffic. We have concluded the operating losses are likely to exceed $625k per month

- for news production services, CHEK management has so far balked at the notion of spending more than the amount they were assuming. We now know the costs will be significantly in excess of that amount.

- we have not resolved the issue of the equipment worth ~$750k

I will walk you through the cost ranges tomorrow.
Thanks

FROM: Sandrelli, John
SENT: Wednesday, August 26, 2009 9:42 p.m.

Andrew,

As promised and as we have been discussing as the next step, attached is the revised APA and a comparison to the version of June. I also attach a draft Escrow Agreement.

I will address your points as follows and trust we can make further progress on a call tomorrow:

- we have indicated, and you had requested, a revised APA. You asked that we work from the form from June. We have done that even though this deal has evolved differently. We also reviewed the [CHCH] Hamilton APA which you directed us to encouraging us to utilize what we could. We are now much closer than we were. If you now require something in a different form, please prepare it for consideration. Alternatively, we would be pleased to finalize the issues in the APA with a view to having it signed.

- our clients are working on the funds. We will explain to you the mechanism for dealing with the escrow when we speak.

- on operational losses, we are still awaiting your figures and our client is confident the amounts can be managed.

- for news, again, we need to know what the numbers are.

- on the $750k as you refer to it, the deal was and is $1 for the assets including existing equipment. If the deal is no longer intended to be $1 please confirm as Canwest has been clear publicly throughout that $1 was the price. Our client will not pay for Canwest to acquire other equipment.

Two minutes after sending this last note to Akman, Sandrelli wrote to Pollard, Germain, and Sampson: "[Akman] is making it hard." The next morning, though, the lawyer suggested a strategy that ultimately won the day: "We may have to submit a binding offer, then go public," wrote Sandrelli. "That involves having the entire $2.5 million with us in escrow."

Upon receiving this message from Sandrelli on Thursday, August 27, Rob Germain sent an urgent email to all CHEK staff letting them know it was time to get the money they had pledged into a trust account—and they had two hours to do it.

"There was a mass exodus—people going to the bank and moving money left, right, and centre," said Bill Pollock. "It was really quite comical. It was all through the Bank of Montreal, and everybody in the bank was a CHEK employee giving them money. The girls behind the counter were going, 'What's going on? What's going on?' And we're like, 'Well, we can't tell you but here's my money, here's my money.' That was pretty funny."

While employees were scrambling to deposit their money, Sandrelli continued his email dialogue with Canwest, now conversing with corporate lawyer Richard Leipsic. Under a veneer of politesse, the lawyers discussed "very significant issues" to be overcome if the sale were to happen. In his final note to Sandrelli, Leipsic wrote: "It [is] extremely difficult for me to recommend going forward."

Still, five hours later, at 5:15 p.m. on August 27, John Sandrelli sent the CHEK employees' official bid for the station to Leipsic and Akman in an email titled, "RE: Victoria APA—Attached Executed Offer":

We enclose the Agreement duly executed which is being submitted for consideration and hopefully for acceptance . . .

The offer is for $2 plus 100% coverage of the operating losses which will be cash collateralized under the escrow. It does not include an additional sum for non-operating losses and our client would request that it have an opportunity to convince the lenders that such is unnecessary and unreasonable.

There are now funds on deposit totaling close to $2.5 million . . . Thank you for your time. We will make ourselves available around the clock to work out any issues you may have.

The employees' offer to buy the station was supposed to have been the top story on CHEK News at 5 o'clock that evening, "but we had to bump it down in the newscast because we hadn't sent [the letter] yet," said Germain. As soon as Sandrelli hit "send," the story went to air.

"We made the offer, even though we knew they were going to reject it . . . There was maybe one last chance that if they rejected it, it would allow for some political pressure."

THE REJECTION CAME THE following morning:

FROM: Akman, Andrew
SENT: August 28, 2009 10:54 AM
TO: Sandrelli, John; Leipsic, Richard
CC: Pollard, John; Germain, Rob; Pollock, Bill; Sampson, Levi
SUBJECT: RE: VICTORIA APA—ATTACHED EXECUTED OFFER

Dear John,

We acknowledge receipt of the Local Investor Group's revised Asset Purchase Agreement in executed form together with a draft unexecuted escrow agreement.

We appreciate you and your clients' extraordinary commitment over the past several weeks, and your efforts to respond to certain of the business and legal issues identified by Canwest.

Regrettably, after giving your clients' revised submission serious consideration, the terms and conditions remain unacceptable . . .

Despite the best efforts of everyone involved, your clients have failed to provide a deposit in the amount required [$5 million] . . .

When we entered into discussions with your clients, it was understood by all that we were up against an immovable deadline of August 31. Regrettably, the timing has worked against our best intentions and efforts.

In light of the station's pending closure on Monday, August 31, Canwest is no longer able to pursue this transaction and negotiations with the Local Investor Group are now terminated.

Canwest must now turn its time and attention to the orderly shut down of the station.

Immediately upon receiving the rejection notice, Pollard, Germain, and Pollock met with all the staff to assure them this was expected—and they would use the quick rejection to their advantage with the media, the public, politicians, and policy makers. In fact, had Canwest waited until Monday, August 31, to reply, CHEK would not have had time for what sales rep Howard Harding later called one last "hail Mary pass at the 11th hour."

Over the next seventy-two hours, CHEK management, Levi Sampson, Gary Lunn, CHEK's lawyers, and CRTC representatives mobilized for one final push. What they achieved during the weekend of August 28 to 30, 2009, has been called "the impossible" by almost everyone involved.

ON FRIDAY, AUGUST 28, Canwest's rejection of the employees' bid to buy the station was the top story on CHEK's evening news. In her news piece, reporter Mary Griffin featured a number of local politicians speaking out on behalf of CHEK. "What they need is an ounce of cooperation from Canwest," said Gary Lunn in the news story, adding, "I'll continue to put pressure on Canwest to see if we can make this happen." Three Island mayors added their voices to the story. "Frankly, I'd like them to reconsider," said Victoria mayor Dean Fortin. Then-BC premier Gordon Campbell also wished CHEK employees well in their efforts: "I hope they are successful," he said.

The following day, even as efforts to save the station were under way, newspapers across the country published news of the employees' rejection. Ironically, the focus of most of the articles—based on a *National Post*/Canwest wire story—was an announcement that Canwest had "won another extension from its senior lenders on a deadline to come up with a recapitalization plan." The news about CHEK running out of time was added as a tag to the story.

In the Saturday, August 29, edition of the *Times Colonist*, Darron Kloster wrote a more thorough account, noting that despite the rejection from Canwest, CHEK employees weren't giving up:

> "This thing isn't over yet," said Richard Konwick, spokesman for the 40 employees at CHEK-TV. "We are continuing discussions with Canwest, the federal government and the CRTC and we firmly believe we have a plan that is viable to stay open."

However, a Canwest spokesman said the media company, which also owns the *Times Colonist*, was not prepared to fund the operation beyond Monday and will close the station after the late newscast. "Canwest cannot assume the risk for costs that may be incurred" under the proposed employee-owned model, John Douglas, vice-president of public affairs, said from Winnipeg. "That includes operating losses, replacement services and other costs." . . .

Douglas said with no programming or advertising inventory in place, "the losses would be significant . . . in the millions" and Canwest was not prepared to absorb debt.

Konwick, however, believes the $2.5 million raised would be "more than enough" to run the station during the broadcast licence transfer. Canwest offered the station for $2 but wanted $5 million as assurance to operate while the licence was transferred, according to Konwick. "That's far, far beyond any operating costs this station has ever used in a 90-day period in the 50-year history of the station."

Days before CHEK got its rejection letter from Canwest, it was rejected by two other significant players—potential financiers Michael O'Connor and Tom Harris. "Tom and I were keen on staying in on the deal—and would have—except the number Canwest was asking for to purchase [$5 million] was ridiculous," said O'Connor. "It seemed to me that Canwest really didn't want the station to be operated. I really believe that the asking price was so high that it was not economically feasible or viable for the employees and a handful of investors, of which I wanted to be one, to buy it at that price. As it came down to the short strokes, they weren't budging at all, and it was not a viable proposition. So Tom and I basically were out of it as it proceeded to closure."

Without financial backing from O'Connor and Harris, the CHEK group would certainly fall short of the $2.5 million it had offered up to Canwest.

Two weeks earlier, though, when the media had first reported that CHEK employees were looking at buying the station, Germain received a number of calls "out of the blue" from people wanting to invest. Some of them were "just kooky," he said, but others had merit.

One serious expression of interest had come from developer and former NHL hockey player Len Barrie, at that time CEO and majority shareholder in the Bear Mountain real estate development and golf course near Victoria. Barrie's colleague, Gerald Hartwig, had called Germain and said, "Len would be interested in putting some money into [CHEK]—a million dollars—and he also said he's got a building up on Bear Mountain that he would be willing to make available to you rent-free."

At the time, the investor group had passed on Barrie's offer, but said they would call if need be. When O'Connor and Harris backed out at the last minute, Levi Sampson contacted Barrie. After reviewing the business plan, Barrie agreed to invest $250,000—but when it came time to put the deposit money in the bank, he missed the deadline, leaving the CHEK group in the lurch. Two other investors who had pledged to come in with Barrie opted out at the same time, taking their collective $500,000 with them, said John Pollard. By this point, too, the CHEK group had deemed Barrie's rent-free space at Bear Mountain unsuitable for a TV station.

With no time to spare, Germain contacted another of the "out-of-the-blue" callers from earlier that summer, insurance company owner Graham Barnes. Germain asked if he was still interested in investing. He was. Barnes met with Pollard—and contributed $500,000 to CHEK—the following day.

Unlike the others in the original investor group, Levi Sampson never wavered in his commitment to the Victoria TV station. "It mattered to me to save the station and keep the jobs here in BC and on the Island," he said. "As long there was a business case to be made for it, I didn't see any reason why I wouldn't try. These people came to me with a lot of hope, and everything I asked of them, they stepped up and met every hurdle. So I felt I would stand by them and try to make an honest go of it."

Even after Canwest rejected the group's offer, Sampson "was right on the front lines of those negotiations," helping to get Canwest back to the table over that final weekend. "We were up against some pretty tight timelines that almost came and went," he said.

By Friday, August 28, 2009, Canwest and the CHEK Media Group appeared to have reached a stalemate. Publicly, Canwest said discussions regarding the sale of the station were over. "Senior vice-president of public affairs John Douglas denied emphatically that there was any hope a deal could still be reached," wrote Keith Vass in the *Saanich News*, a community newspaper in Greater Victoria. "'We are no longer pursuing this transaction. The negotiations with the local investor group are now terminated,' he said."

But the CHEK group insisted that negotiations were continuing. "There are people we are talking to," said Richard Konwick, as quoted in a *Times Colonist* article. "I can't say who it is or how those negotiations are being conducted."

In fact, Douglas and Konwick were both correct. As of that morning, negotiations with Canwest—the corporation—had ceased. But behind-the-scenes conversations between Gary Lunn and Leonard Asper continued, as did consultations between the CRTC and CHEK. Ultimately, these private discussions would bring Canwest back to the table.

Having grown up on Vancouver Island, the CRTC's regional commissioner for BC and Yukon, Stephen Simpson, "understood [CHEK's] relevance to the Vancouver Island marketplace." In addition, "I was quite dismayed that if [the CHEK bid] failed, Victoria would be a provincial capital—the only one, actually—to not have its own television station serving its market.[5] And for those reasons, I felt it was worth us upping the ante and getting involved."

For Simpson, upping the ante meant offering "some good guidance" and "open[ing] up an express line" to help CHEK. "Our real concern was not whether CHEK could make a go of it—because that's just the facts of market life," he said. "It was really that the public deserved to have a local television station, and they were who we were really working for."

With that in mind, on the evening of Friday, August 28, Simpson asked for help on CHEK's behalf from higher up in the CRTC. He contacted then-CRTC chair Konrad von Finckenstein, who had just returned from vacation. Upon hearing this news, Rob Germain sent an email update to Levi Sampson to let him know the CRTC was on CHEK's side: "Canwest has rejected the bid, which we had anticipated. The good thing is the rejection has triggered the powers that be in the CRTC and the Federal Heritage Ministry to consider taking the extraordinary measure of transferring the licence on a provisional basis to CHEK."

While Germain continued to work with Simpson and the CRTC, John Pollard sent a final pitch, "a seven-point plan," to Leonard Asper via email. "What was it going to hurt?" said Pollard. "I was done on Monday. I'd been laid off like everyone else."

In the August 29 email, Pollard laid out his plan, hoping to convince Asper to help the CHEK group reach its goal. He wrote, in part:

> Here is how I see a chance of this working. We already have agreement on much of the APA. Expenses are the main hurdle but I think this will clear that up . . .
>
> CRTC [is] willing to fast track this. We have a schedule approved and our business plan submitted . . .
>
> We pay all of our expenses going forward. Our operating expense budget for year one is 5.9 million dollars. We have 2.5 million in trust and our LPIF is 2.4 million. With zero sales (I will not let that happen) we would lose 1 million dollars (a small risk) . . . A huge news release is issued pointing out how the Asper family made all of this possible at the 11th hour.
>
> The main issue seems to be the exposure to Canwest financially. I do not understand how this has gotten off the rails. We will pay all CHEK related expenses. Simple as that. We have programming that we can air starting at 10 pm on Monday. Worst case it will be a sign saying "The new CHEK NEWS is Under Construction" (but it can be Canadian, local and very average for the first few days). I have the process in place to supply programs for our new schedule within days.
>
> I appreciate that there is little time to spare. This is possible and with a little pushing from you we can make this happen.

Asper quickly replied:

I would caution that you assume any chance of us changing course now is 1 per cent at best. This is not simple and too many people have to be convinced to do something different than planned. Our company is in several sets of negotiations on the larger restructuring, we have lost a few people so the rest are working overtime. This is a complete distraction, and one which is making me pretty unpopular internally.

That said, I will give this some time and attention this weekend. Don't get your hopes up, though. And for sure the last thing that can happen here is for the media to start mentioning my name. So this email has to be entirely confidential. I will shut down instantly if the media start talking about this.

Pollard, heartened by Asper's comments, responded: "1% is still better than yesterday."

That afternoon, Germain received an update from Stephen Simpson that von Finckenstein "has committed to rule on a CHEK transfer of licence application within '30 days or less,' instead of the usual 4–6 months." That significantly lowered Canwest's financial risk, said Germain. "It removed any argument the $2.5 million wouldn't cover operational losses prior to the licence transfer. It also sent a strong signal to Canwest that the CRTC wanted this deal done."

For von Finckenstein, having another local TV station close on his watch wasn't an option. "We [the CRTC] don't want to see stations go dark ever, and certainly not local stations which provide a lot of local content," he said in a 2013 interview. "We had already seen one such station go dark in Brandon and another one in Red Deer."

At the same time, he said, the CRTC had been impressed with the hyper-local model CHCH in Hamilton had created "to resuscitate itself . . . and there was no reason why that couldn't work in the West as well. The CHEK people were trying desperately to put something together. They'd talked to CHCH, and they'd gotten a lot of good advice from them. They were trying to do the same thing."

With that in mind, von Finckenstein advised Simpson to do whatever was necessary to support the CHEK group, including eliminating Canwest's contention that CRTC approval would take too long.

"That's when I instructed Steve specifically to tell them we can do it on a dime. We can turn it around in thirty days if need be. . . . I said let's make sure that [the sale] doesn't falter because of our bureaucratic ineptitude or slowness, or because we're being used as an excuse for not being able to rescue it."

Von Finckenstein also had a persuasive chat with the powers that be at Canwest, knowing they would be appearing before the CRTC on other matters in the coming months. He wanted them to know the CRTC was keen on seeing CHEK survive and that it would be in Canwest's best interests to get back to the bargaining table with the Victoria station. "We didn't want to see CHEK go down like Red Deer," said von Finckenstein. "Whatever solution Canwest had for [its future] would need our approval, and it would be very difficult to obtain it if our approval was for a deal that saw CHEK die. That was the key message, and they got it loud and clear."

Having said that, von Finckenstein also pointed out that while the CRTC wanted to rescue CHEK, it was not prepared to do so at the expense of the bigger-picture Canwest Global deal:

> We were interested in seeing, at all costs, Global survive and the Global stations not being broken up into disparate pieces. [If that happened], that would mean we would only have one national private network, and it would be unlikely that [a second private network] would be reconstructed.
>
> At the same time, we were very interested in seeing CHEK survive—and fortunately it did—but it was a balancing act to make sure that by saving CHEK, we wouldn't upset . . . the sale of all of Global. So my priority was let's keep the Global network sold, or restructured, as one piece. The second one was to make sure that CHEK survived. But let's not have the tail wag the dog—save CHEK and destroy Global.
>
> Lots of people said, "Look, don't touch it. You're just going to screw up the salvage of Global. You can't have that." But [the two goals] were not necessarily incompatible.
>
> But it was difficult. For Leonard . . . he was so busy doing everything that the last thing he needed was that headache on

Vancouver Island. By focusing on CHEK, it made the big deal for them much [riskier]. The lenders said we want [Canwest Global] completely free of everything, we don't want an ongoing liability. So at the CRTC, our focus was very much to make sure that Global survived and also that CHEK survived, but clearly the priorities were 1-2. And if you pushed CHEK too hard, you ran the danger that you'd screw up the big deal.

On Sunday, August 30, Simpson confirmed in writing to CHEK "that upon an agreement for sale and our receipt of your completed application for transfer of ownership, the CRTC will be able to process the application and render a decision within 30 days."

ON THE MORNING OF Thursday, August 27, before he received CHEK's offer to purchase the station, Andrew Akman advised his Canwest colleagues via email that the CHEK group had "consistently demonstrated an unwillingness and/or inability to meet us on our non-negotiable terms, while consuming [a] significant amount of our operational resources as we try to accommodate them in good faith."

With that, Canwest executives agreed to kill the deal immediately and begin the process of shutting CHEK down. A few hours later, though, during a conference call between Canwest and CHEK, Akman inadvertently gave the CHEK group a glimmer of hope, something for which he was later chastised. Another Canwest exec who had participated in the conference call told Akman he should have closed down all discussion, once and for all, at that point. The email exchange between these two Canwest players illustrated the group's state of mind at the time, said Asper.

"They were just tuckered out," he said. "So the idea of stopping everything and engaging in a mad rush to do a last-minute deal was—while from a human perspective appealing—quite unappetizing when stacked up against the other pressures they were facing."

By this time, though, Akman was beginning to see potential—and CHEK took advantage of the window of hope he'd given them. That evening, the CHEK Media Group sent its bid for the station.

The following morning, as Canwest executives and lawyers were drafting a reply refusing CHEK's offer, Gary Lunn called Leonard Asper, asking questions that launched further dialogue among the Canwest players. Even as Canwest sent its rejection letter to CHEK—and as the Victoria group made it clear it wasn't giving up—attitudes began to shift and possibilities began to emerge within Canwest.

Akman, the man the CHEK team had viewed as its arch nemesis, started to "get creative," at this point, said Asper. On Saturday, August 29, Akman proposed what he called an "off-the-wall idea," a complicated shift in CHEK-Canwest management, ownership, and payroll structure. Although the idea never came to fruition, it illustrated Akman's softening stance. "Andrew [went] from being really negative to proposing Hail Mary plans," said Asper who, later that same day, suggested to Canwest insiders that perhaps CHEK had a proposal that "makes sense," and maybe "we should listen."

Even more Canwest naysayers turned pro-CHEK and started to work creatively to come up with a way to get the deal done the following day, when the CRTC announced it would expedite the CHEK transfer-of-licence process and CHEK sent a revised Asset Purchase Agreement. Chris McGinley, who had delivered news of the station's pending shutdown to CHEK staff a month earlier, began lobbying for CHEK. Akman worked out a "Management Buy-Out Cost Benefit Analysis" that showed how the sale of the station to the CHEK employee group could work for Canwest. "Akman [was] still trying to save the day," while Canwest lawyer Richard Leipsic remained "the wet blanket," remembered Asper, who continued his private talks with Sandrelli through it all. "[Sandrelli] would tell me what the problem was from our end, and I would go try to fix it."

As the weekend progressed, and a sale began to become realistic, even Leipsic changed his stance. "There was a time when he was the enemy—and I say this as someone who's his good friend, and I do a lot of work with him, today," said Asper. "But he had become a prisoner of this 'kill-CHEK-at-all-costs' thing. And then he turned at the end, too, and helped get it done—or at least when he thought we had something he thought he could sell to the bondholders. He at least did that. When push came to shove at the right time, he did the right things."

For many at Canwest, doing right by CHEK became a driving force during that final weekend, a way of thumbing their collective noses at the bondholders who had been running their lives for months. Said Asper:

There was this moment at Canwest when we—especially the executive group, who had been doing whatever the bondholders wanted—finally there was this liberating point where we could say, "Screw this. We're going to get this done in a way that they won't approve on the face of it, but when they see the deal, they will approve it." There was this moment when, if music could play, you know in a movie where the ship is sinking and then suddenly somebody finds a way to plug the leak . . .

It was just this moment where we felt like we were just going to do something good for somebody for once. For nine months we'd been forced to cancel contracts or negotiate our way out of this or that, and deal with these guys every two weeks holding a bomb over our heads. It was just this great moment . . . Everybody felt they'd done the right thing and felt really great about it.

With Asper and others at Canwest now pushing for the sale to happen and the CRTC willing to expedite the process, thereby invalidating the bondholder's financial concerns, Andrew Akman, on behalf of Canwest, resumed negotiations with John Pollard and company in Victoria at 7:00 a.m. on Monday, August 31—the day CHEK had been slated to fade to black.

EVEN THOUGH ALL PARTIES were willing to come to the table and negotiations set to resume, the sale of the station still wasn't in the clear, said the CRTC's Stephen Simpson. "When I heard from John [Pollard] that a deal was imminent, everybody was ready to pop the champagne corks, except for one thing. We had a technical problem in our [CRTC] policy. The complication was this," he said:

> If there's a change in ownership, there has to be first an application through Industry Canada for a transfer of the licence —a physical broadcasting licence—to broadcast over the air. The licence we [CRTC] issue is a licence to *operate*, but the applicant first has to have what they call a TA or a "technical acceptance" of the transfer of ownership, because the government takes the ownership of a transmitter very seriously, as all governments do. They want to know who it is that has the right to broadcast something over public airwaves. Industry Canada is very precise and very strict about this process—and that process can take six months.

Because Canwest wanted absolutely no ties with CHEK beyond August 31, it meant that "CHEK, the new owners, would be in possession of a transmitter and the ability to use it without Industry Canada's approval—and that would be against the law, or at least the broadcasting policy of Industry Canada," said Simpson. "And that's where it got really sticky, because without that, they couldn't accept the station, even if Canwest paid them to take it."

Simpson phoned von Finckenstein, who consulted with colleagues to find a way to deal with the situation, making sure it "went down cleanly."

What von Finckenstein did was let the people at Industry Canada know how close CHEK and Canwest were to making this deal, to saving this Vancouver Island television station. He also let them know that Industry Canada was the only thing standing in the way of this deal at this moment. "I said, you must find a way of doing this," said von Finckenstein. "If this doesn't happen right now, then in effect, you end up owning it. You own the failure of CHEK." He told Industry Canada that CHEK, Canwest, and the CRTC had found a way to make the sale happen, and it would be a good idea if "this technical TA business" did not stand in the way at this late date. "I don't know what happened at Industry, but when I made it clear that they would own this failure, they came up with a solution."

That solution involved putting everything related to the CHEK sale—the deposit money and all assets and facilities, including transmitters—into escrow with a known broadcaster. That met the New York bondholders' requirement that the station was off the books *completely*, and it allowed CHEK to continue operations until the CRTC approved the transfer of licence.

John Pollard enlisted Toronto-based James Macdonald, former president of WIC, to become the station's short-term trustee. "We put the transmitter in his name, and Canwest kept the licence," said Pollard. "But the deal was, once we put our application in . . . Canwest no longer had any responsibility towards it."

With that solution in the works, representatives from Canwest and CHEK spent August 31 ironing out details of the APA. "We basically got to about 4 o'clock," recalled Pollard, "and at 4 o'clock, we'd made enough progress that [Canwest] said, 'OK, we'll keep you on the air until Friday.'"[6]

With news of a reprieve, Germain immediately contacted the satellite and cable providers to make sure they kept CHEK on Channel 6 as talks continued. "They had already reassigned the channel," he said, adding, "Telus had jumped the gun and taken us off the air Monday morning."

Late that afternoon, Pollard, Germain, and Pollock broke the news of the imminent deal to staff—and announced it to the public on the evening news. "It was right down to the wire," said Simpson. "It was just right out of a Ron Howard movie, where it was literally the last day, and they were having the public come down and have a big goodbye party for the station, and everything came through in the eleventh hour. It was really dramatic."

By the time the 5 o'clock news started, hundreds of people had gathered in the CHEK parking lot to celebrate the station's fifty-three years on the air. Partygoers didn't know if this was to be a goodbye party or a celebration—until the outdoor newscast started, and anchor Scott Fee announced: "There has been a development in the closure of CHEK News. We will be on the air tomorrow."

FOREIGN OWNERSHIP

In the summer of 2009, the American lenders who held the Canwest debt appeared to be directing the sale of CHEK, dictating to Canwest executives what they could and could not do with the station. Some at CHEK questioned whether it was legal under CRTC regulations for American creditors to be directing the sale of a Canadian company. In fact, the CHEK group was prepared to pose this question publicly if need be, to further pressure Canwest into "doing the right thing" and selling the station to employees.

It never came to that, and in a 2013 interview, former CRTC chair Konrad von Finckenstein clarified the situation: "Once you are in a bankruptcy situation or near bankruptcy, it doesn't make a difference whether it's a Canadian or foreign lender. It's the lender who calls the tune because after all, they have certain legitimate rights."

But, he added, those lenders still have rules to follow. "They didn't really control [the sale of Canwest assets] except to the extent that they had control of the *process* of disposal within the rules. The rules say clearly that you have to dispose of it to Canadians. But how to do that, the timing, etcetera, that was all in their hands . . . So they controlled the fact that it had to be sold by Leonard [Asper], but not who would get it."

In a *Winnipeg Free Press* News Café interview in February 2013 with reporter Geoff Kirbyson, Asper explained the demise of Canwest from his perspective, starting at the moment the banks got nervous about Canwest's falling profits:

> In the world of high finance, what happens is the banks sell off your loan to a bunch of guys called hedge funds, and these hedge funds, their business is to take your company from you. They actually don't want to lend you the money. They want to call your loan and push you out

. . . continued on next page

and take over the company because they believe it's a good company. They'll then sell the company and make a bunch of money, which is exactly what happened . . .

The headlines were that [Canwest] was going under, but what was really going on was that there was a chess match going on, or a war going on, for control of the company between [shareholders and] creditors, who were using the right they had to call the loan to try to push the shareholders out. The board of directors was put in a very difficult position. They [the hedge fund managers] were putting guns to our heads. They kept giving us extensions, two weeks at a time . . . threatening to put the company into a receivership position.

At the time, in the bondholders' minds, CHEK was already off the books. Bringing it back into the discussion in August 2009 took focus away from the bigger Canwest Global deal that was in play at the time. The bondholders' goal was to eliminate all expenses or liabilities—including CHEK. "It's raw capitalism at work," said Asper in an interview. "There's no soul to it. It's pure math . . . It just becomes full plunder, and they [the bondholders, in this case] don't care about the aftermath because they'll be gone." ■

The next day, the *Times Colonist* reported on the station's reprieve:

Cheers greeted the announcement, made on the 5 p.m. newscast, which was broadcast from what might have been a goodbye party in CHEK's parking lot off Kings Road . . . "We're going to have to take it one day at a time," said CHEK general manager John Pollard. "We need an agreement and with a little bit of luck we'll have it."

Canwest, the Canadian Radio-television and Telecommunications Commission, different levels of government, and employees are working on the plan, Pollard said. "Buying a TV station isn't like buying a car. You've got lots of stuff to do and that's what we are working our way through right now," he said . . .

John Douglas, vice-president of communications for Canwest, said yesterday that a revised proposal from the investor group addresses deficiencies in the earlier bid, and includes taking responsibility for all costs during an interim period. "This is an important step for us because for seven months we've been saying that we weren't prepared to assume that financial risk during that period of time," Douglas said. "Our goal would be to have everything finalized by Friday. It would be a framework that would allow it to move forward for CRTC approval . . . There still is a great deal of work to do and we are still looking to do in days what would normally take months."

Over the next four days, as Pollard, Pollock, and the lawyers continued working through the APA with Canwest, CHEK staff scrambled to fill airtime, as described by Germain:

We ended up pulling out of our own archives . . . [shows] that were from five or ten years ago, but were still watchable and weren't going to cost us any money. We started airing those at various times throughout the day, and augmented it with [shows] that Canwest provided to us, things they had on the shelf that they weren't airing anywhere else. But they did actually charge us for it, and they charged us a fair amount for it.

We had [a few] ads. We were airing the same ads over and over again and PSAs. And everyone in the newsroom did [testimonials] to camera, like "I'm so-and-so. I'm an employee-owner. Thanks for watching CHEK. Thanks for supporting CHEK."

Those were running throughout the day as well, just to augment commercial breaks. We had to fill up time. Those are ways we filled it from going to black.

Negotiations continued until Friday, September 4, in what *Maclean's* reporter Jason Kirby called "one of the zaniest weeks in Canadian TV history. In the span of just four days, the two sides scrambled to hammer out a mammoth licence-transfer agreement, numbering in the hundreds of pages and covering every transmitter, camera and chair in the place."

On September 4, 2009, Leonard Asper sent an email to all Canwest employees:

> I'm pleased to say that today we reached an agreement to sell CHEK-TV in Victoria to a local investor group that includes nearly all its local employees . . . It's unusual to "celebrate" the sale of a station but given the circumstances and the odds that have been overcome and particularly the effort required by many people at Canwest, I believe that this is worth celebrating. Everyone is better off for the result that we achieved today.

That same day, Asper penned a note in his personal files, saluting the success of the CHEK deal and the fact that so many people had worked together to "find a way out of an impossible situation, saving 45 jobs, saving Canwest about $1 million in severance (by not having to fire people) and keeping a news source alive. When I look back I will cherish it as a great personal leadership moment." It was particularly satisfying, he wrote, given all the negativity surrounding Canwest at the time. "In all the pile of manure we are in, this was a diamond."

That afternoon, vice-president Chris McGinley—who, six weeks earlier, had delivered the news the station would be closed—wrote to all CHEK staff:

> I will forever remember July 22nd, when I visited the station and announced that . . . the station would be shut down. Even when faced with the toughest of news, management and staff never lost hope, and quickly moved toward finding a solution of their own.
>
> What we have seen over the last number of weeks is the same tenacity and focus that has reverberated throughout the history of CHEK . . .

Congratulations! Celebrate your accomplishment knowing that I and all your Canwest colleagues wish you the very best and will be raising a glass to your success tonight.

While CHEK management and staff, Stephen Simpson, and Gary Lunn all credit each other—and Leonard Asper and the Greater Victoria community—with saving the station, they all agree that good luck and good timing also played a role. Richard Konwick summed up the events of the summer of 2009 as follows:

> If any one of the players in this whole chain of events had not done what they did, it would have derailed. It's an unbelievable cast of characters and events that came together to create the conditions for this.
>
> Essentially, you had to go out every day and flip a coin, and it had to come up heads. And that gave you the chance to flip it again the next day. If it ever came up tails, it was over.
>
> It's mind-blowing . . . and when you tell the story, even in the abbreviated form, people's mouths just drop open. They cannot believe what happened.

seven

INDEPENDENCE DAYS (2009–12)

Though buying a TV station for a few dollars might seem like a low-risk proposition, the new owners must be able to install the necessary infrastructure, such as advertising sales departments, functions which would previously have been supplied by the parent company. They must be able to absorb early losses: commercial revenue has cratered because advertisers were reluctant to buy time on a station slated to close.

—**Grant Robertson,** *Globe and Mail,* August 31, 2009

AFTER JOHN POLLARD, NOW president of the CHEK Media Group, signed off on the final piece of the Asset Purchase Agreement, all that remained was for CHEK to pay for the television station it had just purchased.

"I got the vice-president of Global BC, Brett Manlove, to give our lawyers [in Vancouver] the two bucks to pay," said Pollard. "I wasn't over there to give them the toonie that had to change hands. I think I actually borrowed the money from Brett, so I guess he's part owner . . . I don't think I ever paid him back."

With that, the celebrations began.

But the following day, a new reality set in, said Dana Hutchings, who now added assistant news director to her roster of roles at the station:

In a lot of ways, we felt that the feat was buying [the station] and keeping it open. But I think the next day, there was [a sense of] "What do we have to do now?" Keeping it open was so much the focus. And now we're open. Great. We have no programming. We have no commercials. We have nothing. We all thought we could rest, but now the work begins. It turned into, "We don't get to relax. We have to keep going."

Or, as operations manager Bill Pollock said, "The good news is we bought a TV station. The bad news is we bought a TV station."

The day it became independent, CHEK and its employee-owners began rebuilding. They needed more staff. They needed a control room, master control, and a news studio. They needed programming, advertisers, and equipment—and they still needed the CRTC's stamp of approval.

On November 9, 2009, nine weeks after CHEK finalized its dealings with Canwest, the CRTC awarded the Victoria station a seven-year licence, the maximum allowed. Even though the CRTC had promised to expedite the application, "we didn't know if they would give us a licence or not . . . until [we] actually got the document," said Pollock. "When we got the licence, it certainly took a lot of pressure off."

Television 101: In Control In a TV station, the control room is where all the elements of a single, often live, show are mixed and managed. During a newscast, for example, a director, producer, and audio expert are among the people who work in a control room.

Master control, on the other hand, is where *everything* a television station puts on air is monitored—local shows, purchased programming, and commercials. Master control is staffed by at least one operator twenty-four hours a day to make sure everything runs on time and according to broadcast regulations.

Meanwhile, CHEK had already started hiring new staff. At the time of the sale, it had thirty-three full- and part-time employees—"not enough to run a television station," said senior producer Richard Konwick. Within its first few months as an employee-owned entity, CHEK hired new advertising salespeople, commercial producers, control room staff, and master control operators, increasing its total staff to about seventy-five people.

The first person hired back was director of creative services Michael Woloshen, who had been laid off in 2008 after almost three decades at CHEK. "When the opportunity came to jump in again, I jumped in," he said. "It seemed to be a good gamble. The work needed to be done. There was a lot of commercial production work . . . and they needed someone to help coordinate that. It was a no-brainer for me."

Because CHEK's structure was now unique in the Canadian television market, and because most of the employees (all but management) were still union members, the Victoria CEP unit's union contract had to change. For example, because outside investors were not willing to take on the liability of a pension plan, "we had a one-day meeting, where we re-opened the contract, deleted that clause, and signed a new contract with Canwest prior to the sale," said Konwick, CHEK's union president.

Later, the union and management agreed to add a clause to the collective agreement stating that all new employees were required to buy into the company. At first, the buy-in for new full-time employees was $15,000, an amount later reduced to $5,000. "The only way we could legally compel people to do that was to put it in the [union] contract, saying that as a condition of employment, you are required to buy shares."

Given that everyone who worked at CHEK—management and unionized staff—were now co-owners of the company, "the other thing that is written into the contract," Konwick added, "is a whole section on the Joint Union-Management Committee. That compels management to sit down with elected union representatives—not the president of the local but people who are elected by their peers to sit on this committee to discuss the issues around the company . . . It's very much an industrial democracy kind of model where people have their say in the running of the company."

That's not to say a hierarchy no longer existed after the employees purchased the station. "For the most part, it operates like any business," said Konwick. "The people who are in charge are in charge, and the people who do the work do the work." Having said that, he added that the relationship between unionized staff and management was "night and day," when compared to the days when Canwest ran the company. "There's one layer of management between me and the board of directors—and I'm on the board of directors."

John Pollard, Rob Germain, and Bill Pollock, who were managers under Canwest, continued to lead the day-to-day station operations, albeit with some role changes. Pollard's title changed from general manager to president; Pollock added program manager to his existing job as operations manager; and Germain, who remained news director in title, took on more station-wide responsibilities. The CHEK Media Group also promoted two others to management when it purchased the station—Tanya Smith, manager of community relations, and Peggy Heyer, manager of human resources and accounts payable. This five-member leadership group was now "the top of the rung," said Pollock. "If there needs to be a decision made, this is it. You don't have to wait and go down East. We're certainly masters of our own destiny."

That was the upside of the arrangement. The downside was that this management group, and the employees it led, was completely responsible for navigating the challenges of what the media quickly dubbed "an experiment that has never been tried in Canada" and "an experiment in the future of local television."

For the first few months after the sale of the station, Canwest provided CHEK's new owners with "transitional support, such as continuing use of its television control room in Vancouver, programming and a lease for CHEK's Kings Road building at favourable rates," reported the *Times Colonist* in September 2009.

In previous years, in its efforts to cut costs, Canwest had "centralized virtually all aspects of the television station," said Konwick. "The only thing that was left in Victoria was a green screen and robotic cameras—and the anchors were here."

That meant, to produce an in-house newscast, CHEK had to restore its studio, build a set for the news anchors, buy cameras and other equipment, and install a control room and master control facility. Canwest gave the group six months before it planned to pull the plug on the interim arrangements.

GREEN SCREEN

In television, the saying, "the camera doesn't lie" is, in fact, a fib. Sometimes, what the viewer sees isn't what's there at all. Newscast weather reports are perhaps the most common example of this TV trickery.

At home, the viewer might see a weather forecaster standing in front of a map, pointing to high and low systems, cloud covers, and sunny patches. In the studio, though, that weathercaster is actually standing in front of a giant, blank green background, or "green screen," pointing at nothing. The green screen blocks the studio background so that another image, such as a weather map, can be superimposed onto the scene during the broadcast.

It's all physics, related to isolating a single colour hue and making it transparent. Green and blue are the most common background colours used for this purpose because human skin does not come in these colours. If the weather forecaster standing in front of a green screen is wearing a green outfit, though, that outfit will disappear, leaving behind nothing but the forecaster's floating head. ■

"This has got to be one of the most expensive businesses to get into and to maintain," said Pollock. "So we were borrowing and begging for used equipment from Canwest and a couple of other stations. Red Deer [CHCA] had just closed down, so we thought we might be able to get our hands on some of that stuff. We sort of cobbled stuff together just to get us going." CHEK also acquired equipment from CHCH in Hamilton and CHBC (Global) in Kelowna.

When it came to rebuilding the facilities, staff jumped in to help—including new employees who had just been hired to operate the systems now under construction. While one group worked on the control room or master control, another worked on the news studio. "We built our own [news] set for $7,000," said Germain, noting that

Canwest had spent $100,000 on the previous one. "Our graphics designer designed the look of the set and actually built a lot of it himself. He did some of the staining of the wood and things like that. It's a standard, low-tech set-up."

Despite the scrimping and do-it-yourself approach to the rebuilding process, it still cost money, about $1.8 million, which the CHEK group didn't have. "There was zero cash flow," said Konwick. "It became apparent that we had to come up with more money, so we went out to look for more people to buy shares. The [M1 union] unit in Calgary came in with another $100,000. They wanted to see us succeed." Staff, management, and existing private investors also upped their financial contributions.

CHEK launched its new studio, control room, and master control on February 15, 2010, two weeks ahead of Canwest's deadline. "The day we went to air with our first [in-house] newscast, literally, five minutes before air, we had no audio," said Pollock. "We were down to the wire. Three minutes before air, we got it. That's how close it was."

As a stand-alone station, CHEK was now in complete control of its newscasts and programming. "If there's breaking news, we can go on the air any time, day or night," said Germain. Under Canwest, the decision to interrupt existing programming in favour of breaking news wasn't CHEK's call. Back then, if breaking news happened, CHEK had to phone master control in Calgary for permission to go on air. "Often the answer was no because of a program that was on that was too important or too valuable," he said. "Or the control room wasn't available [because] they were doing another show, airing in another time zone. This gives us a lot more flexibility as a news organization."

In the spring of 2011, the CHEK Media Group achieved another major facilities-related milestone when it bought the forty-thousand-square-foot building that housed the station.

"Canwest was under creditor protection for quite a while, and as a result, the building was in limbo," said Germain. Under Canwest ownership, CHEK had paid rent to the parent company but had no control over the station's physical location.

When Shaw acquired Canwest's assets in 2010, the CHEK building was included in the deal. For months, "this real uncertainty hung over our heads." Would Shaw move into the building, sell it, jack up the rent? Would CHEK be forced to relocate? "What scared us the most was how much it would cost to move to a different location," said Germain. "It would have been in the order of $2 million to move. You can't just find a warehouse somewhere and move in. The costs of making that move would be prohibitive."

Eventually, Shaw decided it didn't want the building and offered to sell it to CHEK below market value. By this time, to minimize the rent it had been paying to Canwest, CHEK had already compressed its operations into the building's first floor. That meant the second and third floors were available to rent out.

The board of directors researched the renter-versus-owner business model, and found that if the CHEK group purchased the building, the monthly mortgage payments would be about the same as what the company had been paying in rent. But as owner of the facility, CHEK would have the added option of leasing out the vacant space to boost its bottom line.

Decision made, the CHEK Media Group took possession of the Kings Road building on June 1, 2011.[7]

Within a month of CHEK buying the building, the first paying tenant, a software company, moved in on the third floor. In January 2013, Victoria's CBC Radio relocated from its downtown location into the second floor, space formerly occupied by the CHEK newsroom. The rest of the second floor remains vacant, available to rent to new tenants or to be used by CHEK as expansion space if need be. All tenants share the costs of operating the building—utilities, maintenance, and reception.

To come up with the down payment to buy the building, CHEK raised money "internally and externally," said Germain. "There were more [CHEK] shares issued. I bought some more, and all the employees were given first opportunity if they wanted to add to their shares. You still got the 30 per cent tax credit on it." Unidentified outside investors also contributed.

To Germain, buying the building offered the company a sort of security blanket. "We now had some hard assets that backed up our shares in this company. So if something ever happened to CHEK, the broadcast company, CHEK [the business group] would still own a $6 million building . . . If worse came to worst, we could sell the building for quite a bit more than we purchased it for and enter into a long-term lease with whoever we sold it to."

Developing the site is another down-the-road possibility. The property, which covers almost a full city block of prime real estate, is on a main transportation corridor in an area the City of Victoria has identified as having future high-density potential. "The footprint of the building [covers] a fraction of the land, so you could easily build out where the parking lot is now," said Germain.

IN THE EARLY DAYS of independent ownership, CHEK, having lost all its Canwest programming, scrambled to fill twenty-four hours of airtime every day. "We had nothing, so we could start from scratch," said John Pollard. That meant negotiating for low-priced movies to run in the evenings and paid programming to fill the overnight and early morning hours. The afternoons and early evenings were to be filled with local news in the form of "news wheels," pre-recorded headline news packages that repeated several times an hour. Originally, the news wheels ran for fifteen minutes, four times an hour. That later expanded into a pair of thirty-minute news packages that were replayed throughout the afternoon.

A month after the CHEK Media Group bought the Victoria TV station, *Maclean's* magazine reported on the programming side of CHEK's "new broadcast model":

For starters, CHEK won't enter bidding wars for high-priced American TV shows. Under the old regime, the cost for a season of programing had spiked from $10 million to $25 million over the last five years, making it unprofitable. Instead, CHEK is banking that it can return to profitability with a mix of less expensive, locally produced news programs during the day, and movies at night. "We're not a charity, but we don't have corporate shareholders demanding huge returns," [Pollard] says. Pollard estimates CHEK's revenues will be just 25 to 35 per cent of what they used to be. The flip side is that the station's programming costs will also be just 20 per cent of what they were under Canwest.

To boost revenue, CHEK filled half its available airtime with paid programming. The station began airing the Liquidation Channel (a.k.a. the Shopping Channel) daily from midnight to 6:00 a.m., with religious programming and infomercials running from 6:00 a.m. to noon.

"Some might say it's unsavoury," said Pollard, as quoted by Anna Killen in the *Langara Journalism Review*. "But the first part of 'paid programming' is 'paid,'" noted the writer, who followed up with another comment from Pollard: "It wasn't genius. But it [made] payroll."

Immediately after purchasing the station, Pollard negotiated a movie deal with MGM. He told the distributor that the movies "don't have to be good. They don't have to be new. They have to be edited to fit into a two-hour time block, edited for television and close captioned." MGM's original asking price was $20,000 per title, including permission to air each film twice. Pollard countered, offering to pay $1,500 per title for two plays each. "I said, 'You have these movies. They're just sitting there, and they're just going to sit. Nobody wants them except me.'" Surprisingly, MGM agreed, and CHEK acquired two hundred old movies that aired in evening time slots for the next few years.

In its early days as an independent, CHEK ran a few very inexpensive American network programs. "We didn't have the luxury [to] buy anything we couldn't afford to pay for," said Pollard. "We didn't buy any programs that we knew we were not going to break even on, so we worked with our national, regional, and local [sales] people and said, 'How much can you bring in?' If they couldn't bring in enough to pay for it, we didn't even bid on it."

Gradually, the stock of purchased programming increased to include such shows as *Supernatural, Hart of Dixie, The Insider, 60 Minutes, Jimmy Kimmel Live!, Nightline,* and *48 Hours Mystery.* This rise in CHEK's mainstream programming was thanks, in part, to an arrangement with CHCH in Hamilton, now an independent station owned by Channel Zero. The two former Canwest stations began sharing programming—and programming costs—in the fall of 2010. In addition to American series, the two began sharing sports broadcasts. "We've also run some blockbuster movies that we got through CHCH," said program manager Bill Pollock. For example, "we were the first to run *Avatar,* Hamilton and us. It's those kinds of deals we're constantly agreeing to with them. If it's a specialty movie or a series, they may go and buy it and then say, 'Here's your share. This is what it's going to cost you.' We're always going back and forth."

In the fall of 2012, because of this program-sharing arrangement, the two stations started airing a pair of programs with huge audience appeal—*Jeopardy!* and *Wheel of Fortune.* These shows may be more expensive to buy, but they appeal to national advertisers, meaning they bring in more ad dollars for CHEK and CHCH. "The national sales people can say [to potential advertisers], 'OK, if you buy this, you've got an audience right across the country with these two stations,'" said Pollock.

Ultimately, though, since the CHEK group first bought the station, its goal has been to focus on Vancouver Island, with local news and locally produced specialty shows. At first, "we leaned very heavily" on existing west coast fishing shows, because that's what was in CHEK's archives, said Pollard.

One of the first *new* Island-produced shows to air on CHEK was *Flavours of the West Coast,* a travel and food show that debuted in the fall of 2010. A local sports show, *Game On!,* started soon after—and paid for itself immediately. "[It] developed from a staff idea," wrote Anna Killen in the *Langara Journalism Review.* "They'd been pitching the show to Canwest for four years but were always turned down and told it wouldn't make any money. In its first two weeks, *Game On!* had already paid for the next 52 weeks of programming."

By the fall of 2012, CHEK was airing eight to nine hours a week of non-news, locally produced shows, including travel, design, cooking, seniors, health, and Aboriginal programming.

"We do as much local programming as we [can]," said Pollard. "We think this is what we're supposed to be as a Canadian TV station. We think we're supposed to be a local television station serving the market we're part of. We don't think we should be an American television station with a smattering of Canadian programming. What we do is serve the market we're in."

To further this objective, in its first few years as an employee-owned station, CHEK made space in its schedule to air the work of local, independent documentary producers. "They had nowhere to run their stuff, so we carved out an hour on a Saturday afternoon that was just for documentaries," said Pollock. "There was no charge to them . . . We sat down with the independent film producers and talked to them, and they just kept supplying us. We aired them five or six times apiece."

This dedicated documentary spot is no longer in the regular schedule, but the programming lineup has enough flexibility that, when a good local film comes along, CHEK makes room for it, he said. "One thing about our schedule is we're the ones who created it, so if it needs to get adjusted—other than the simulcast shows we take from Hamilton or from somewhere else—we can move it back and forth. It's a juggling act when you do programming."

ON TUESDAY, SEPTEMBER 1, 2009, the day after the station had been slated to close, CHEK made its first major change to its news programming, moving the late-night newscast to 10:00 p.m. and shortening it to thirty minutes. Under Canwest, the station had run an hour-long newscast at 11:00 p.m. "They needed to fill the [local content] quota," said Rob Germain. "Because we were only doing half an hour at supper, they needed an hour to fill the quota later on. But it doesn't make sense to have an hour-long newscast at 11 o'clock, when people want to catch up and go to bed, and only a half-hour at 5 o'clock."

Canwest had limited CHEK's suppertime cast to thirty minutes to make room for *Global National* at 5:30 p.m. In addition, Canwest's centralized control room only allotted so much time to each of the stations that shared it. "We only had half an hour of control room time," said Germain.

During the fall of 2009, CHEK's newscasts continued to evolve. In early September, independent of the Asset Purchase Agreement negotiations with Canwest, the station's new owners worked out a news-sharing agreement with Canwest to help them through their first six months as an independent. Three months into the agreement, though, Canwest wanted to renegotiate. By this time, the corporation was in creditor protection and working hard to streamline operations. But CHEK was not yet in a position to completely cut its ties with Canwest, so the former parent company instead laid out new terms— and a steeper price—for the news-sharing agreement. Under Canwest's revamped arrangement, CHEK would be permitted to run Global news packages, but only *after* Global had aired them, and Global would be allowed to use any CHEK stories at any time. In addition, CHEK was to pay $120,000 a year for this service.

"Canwest was pretty hard-nosed about it," said Germain. "They made it pretty clear that they saw us as a potential client, buying services from them, rather than as a partner [with] a true sharing agreement. At the time, we were barely making payroll. We weren't in a position to suddenly be paying out dollars that we weren't expecting to pay. So we went looking elsewhere."

Around the same time, veteran Vancouver news anchor Tony Parsons approached CHEK about becoming an investor and an employee of the station.

"I had a place in my heart for CHEK, and I didn't want to see it die," said Parsons in a 2013 interview. "It was the oldest television station in the province. It was sort of a heritage thing, and I thought it would be a shame to just let this thing wither on the vine and suddenly go away. It was popular on the Island. People liked the shows it did, so I thought . . . maybe it would work out if my name was attached to it."

In January 2010, the *Times Colonist* reported on Parsons's move to CHEK:

> Parsons, who anchored the *News Hour* at Global B.C. for 26 years until his departure last month [December 2009], confirmed rumours that he was making a personal investment in the employee-owned television station and expects to be back on the airwaves March 16. His presence is sure to help ratings at CHEK. When he anchored the news at Global, it was the most-watched English-language newscast in Canada . . .
>
> After 50-plus years in broadcasting, Parsons, who was born in 1939, said he wasn't ready to retire. He describes his work as "the most fun you can have without laughing."
>
> When he heard that employees had bought CHEK last year, he was moved to call. "I asked if there was a spot for me," said Parsons. "I saw it as a chance for me to continue my career with people who I know and admire."
>
> Parsons, like every other employee at CHEK, will invest an undisclosed sum of money to be a part-owner of the station.

Shortly after Parsons agreed to work with CHEK, another television station came calling. CBC British Columbia also wanted the veteran newsman. Johnny Michel, CBC's regional director of programming, "resolved to lure Parsons in hopes of boosting CBC's distant-third local news viewership (from around 25,000) and quintupling its advertising revenues," wrote Malcolm Perry in the *Vancouver Sun* in June 2010.

He was too late, though. Parsons told Michel he wasn't available to CBC because he'd already made a commitment to CHEK. But Parsons gave Michel a window of hope when he added that, if CBC could "work something out" with CHEK, he would consider doing the news at both stations.

At the end of January 2010, CBC's Johnny Michel met with CHEK's John Pollard in Victoria to discuss the idea of news sharing between the two broadcasters. At the meeting, Pollard said to Michel, "I need a news sharing agreement, and I don't have one that I'm comfortable with. And it has to be *sharing*. I don't have any money." Michel replied, "OK, I need Tony Parsons."

The two broadcasters ironed out an arrangement that returned CHEK to its roots as an independent station with a CBC affiliation. They began sharing news footage and feeds. They also began sharing Parsons, who started anchoring CHEK's 10 o'clock newscast on March 15, 2010. On April 12, he also became co-host to Gloria Macarenko on *CBC News Vancouver* at 5:00, 6:00, and 6:30 p.m. The *Times Colonist* reported on the arrangement:

> "Nobody's more surprised than me," Parsons said. "I have two jobs, two masters essentially, two contracts and [two] union memberships."
>
> As part of its deal with CHEK, CBC has agreed to share its news content, which will see the Victoria station broadcast *CBC News Vancouver* from 6 to 6:30 p.m.
>
> CHEK news director Rob Germain said the CBC newscast will complement the independent station's flagship 5 p.m. news show with [anchor] Scott Fee. "It will just add to our programming," Germain said. "We are going to be news affiliates of CBC, so we will have access to news feeds from across Canada. And at the same time, we will be providing the CBC with footage and newsgathering on Vancouver Island, and sharing what happens here with people across Canada."

For the first six months of his dual hosting duties, Parsons flew back and forth between Vancouver and Victoria. "In the afternoon, I would fly by helicopter to Vancouver," he said. "I'd be rushed from the helipad downtown and arrive at CBC and do the show for them, and then there would be a taxi waiting for me outside the CBC building at 6:30, and I'd be rushed out to YVR. I'd get on a fixed wing Air Canada plane, and there'd be a taxi waiting on the other side for me, to rush me to CHEK. It was comical in its way, but it was a bit wearing."

Eventually, the two stations set up a studio in the basement of CBC Vancouver, where Parsons could comfortably deliver the 10:00 p.m. CHEK newscast without the travel headaches.

Still, after two years of hosting two newscasts for two different stations in two different cities, seventy-three-year-old Parsons opted out of CHEK's 10:00 p.m. show in June 2012. He continued to appear on CHEK via the *CBC News Vancouver* simulcast at 6:00 p.m. until he retired from CBC in December 2013.

Meanwhile, as soon as CHEK had linked up with CBC and re-established its control rooms in February 2010, it was able to drop *Global National* at 5:30 p.m., increase its local newscast to an hour, and follow up the CBC simulcast with another thirty minutes of Island-based news, beginning at 6:30.

"That's worked out quite well," said Germain in 2012. "CBC appreciates what we offer them, with all the newsgathering resources on Vancouver Island. It's something they didn't have before. They only had the bureau at the [BC] Legislature for TV. They have a radio station here, but video-wise, they just had one photographer. So it was just a win-win for everybody, and the Tony deal was the icing on the cake for them." The national broadcaster further increased its presence in Victoria in September 2012 when CHEK added CBC Vancouver's 11:00 p.m. newscast to its programming schedule.

In its early years as an independent television outlet, CHEK revamped more than just its evening news programming. In the fall of 2010, the station brought back its noon newscast, which Canwest had cut in 2006. The following summer, it further enhanced news production by cancelling *Island 30*, a half-hour local affairs show that had aired for two years.

"Producing a daily show like that was taking a lot of resources, resources that we wanted to plow back into our newscasts and better utilize there," said Germain. "*Island 30* was a good community program, but it wasn't generating the same kinds of ratings. We didn't lay anybody off. We just incorporated all the staff that were dedicated to that show and repurposed them back into news."

Cancelling *Island 30* allowed CHEK to expand its weekend suppertime newscasts from thirty minutes to a full hour, and it allowed salespeople to sell higher-priced ads for the higher-rated news programs.

In terms of newsgathering employees, the numbers haven't changed dramatically since the station became independent. That's because the news department was the only one still fully functional, and fully staffed, in the last days of Canwest ownership. What has changed, though, are the tasks each news employee does. Originally, newsroom employees worked as reporters *or* videographers *or* editors. Now, everyone multitasks, said Germain.

This shift to "one-man bands [who] report, shoot, and edit," started with CHEK's Nanaimo and Comox Valley bureaus, while the station was still owned by Canwest. But after the change of ownership, all newsroom employees began multitasking, "making the newsroom more efficient," said Germain. "Taking advantage of technology makes it a lot easier to do that than it would have been in the past."

Beefing up CHEK's online presence was also an early priority for the new owners. "We realize that that's the future," said Germain, adding that in the spring of 2010, CHEK became the first television station in BC to livestream its newscast. "People want to be able to watch your news on whatever screen they choose, whenever they want, whenever it's convenient for them. That's why we need to be there. I see it as a way of reaching people who aren't traditional television news viewers, reaching those people through the online traffic, and reaffirming the people who are traditional news watchers, and giving them a way to interact with our newscast."

One way CHEK has facilitated this interaction is through a segment titled "CHEK Point," produced by Dana Hutchings. "It's a talkback segment," said Germain. "We're using social media to integrate that with our newscast and trying, on Facebook in particular, to start a discussion every day about a topic of the day."

Today, CHEK's Facebook page is the most "liked" page of all news organizations on Vancouver Island, with almost five times the number of "fans" as its nearest Facebook competitor, the *Times Colonist*. "It's an area we're trying to push," said Germain. "I want CHEK News to be the number one news brand on Vancouver Island period—online, on TV, wherever."

DURING THE SUMMER OF 2009, because it had planned to close CHEK on August 31, Canwest had stopped booking national and regional advertising for the Victoria station. "They had basically taken every lick of business off the books for CHEK, [moving] everything they could, nationally and regionally, onto Global," recalled CHEK president John Pollard in the summer of 2012. "We had no national business, no regional business."

At the same time, new local sales were hard to come by. "A lot of people would say to me, 'Well, come see us if you're still around,'" said sales rep Howard Harding. "The prices were incredibly good. They were like fire sale prices. Summer is a good time to buy TV anyway, but we had further discounted to make it attractive. It was pretty tough to sell the station during that summer."

That said, most longtime local advertisers stood by CHEK. "They were pulling for us during those two difficult months," said Harding. A few, who "couldn't stand the risk," moved to the competition, A-Channel (now CTV Two), while others were *forced* to go to the competition because CHEK no longer had production facilities to create new ads for its clients. One of those forced to move its ad production was Dodd's Furniture, a move that made headlines in Victoria and Vancouver newspapers. On September 3, 2009, the *Times Colonist* reported:

> Gordie Dodd, the furniture store owner known for his cheesy television pitches depicting himself as Spider-Man, the Incredible Hulk and other characters, confirmed yesterday he has shifted production of the commercials over to A British Columbia. Dodd, who has had CHEK-TV produce the spots for 30 years, said he will continue to advertise on both stations.

Come fall 2009, CHEK's stable of advertisers was pretty slim. When the employee group first took over, the station ran existing ads for long-term clients for free to help fill airtime. Before long, though, local ad sales took off, said Harding:

> There was a huge shift as soon as the good news broke, and we bought the station. People [advertisers] were calling in. We rarely have people phone in, calling in and saying, "I'd like to know more about rates." It does happen but it was very

frequent in those early days. We had people walking in, even, and people who would contact us and say, "I never would have dealt with you when you were Canwest, but now that you're independent, I want to talk to you." So there were a lot more potential leads that happened after the sale.

CHEK soon rebuilt its commercial production department, hiring staff and equipping production booths so it could once again create ads for local customers. Gordie Dodd brought his business back to CHEK as soon as the station was able to accommodate him and his elaborate commercials. In those early months, the bulk of CHEK's ad revenues came from local sales, making for an unusual model in the television world, said Pollard:

> The traditional advertising model is agency-based, and 80 to 90 per cent of your business is going to come from advertising agencies in Toronto, Vancouver, Calgary and Montreal. Typically they buy simulcast US programming, of which we had none. So it didn't work.
>
> However, because we'd cut the cost of our programming down dramatically, our overhead wasn't as big as it was under Canwest . . . so we were successful in turning that [traditional advertising] model upside down. We basically went 75 per cent local and 25 per cent agency. Is that a brilliant model? No. But it was survival.

Pollard said CHEK brought in about $50,000 in ad revenue during the first month, but payroll was about $250,000 a month. "So this nest egg that we had put together to run the station was going down dramatically."

To increase local sales, CHEK immediately hired two new ad reps, one of whom was dedicated to mid-Island sales (Ladysmith to Qualicum Beach and Port Alberni). At first, Canwest continued to help CHEK sell ads throughout BC, but the station soon started working with an ad agency in Vancouver. For national sales, CHEK turned to an agency in Toronto, but because agencies consider

CHEK a "tier-two station," they expected it to offer lower prices to potential advertisers. "The problem with agency buys is they tend to negotiate badly and nastily," said Pollard. "Independent TV is tough."

Still, ad sales increased over the months until February 2010, when CHEK recorded its first profit. "And not just any profit," wrote Anna Killen in the *Langara Journalism Review*. "CHEK Media Group cleared a whopping 250 bucks." She quoted Pollard: "Of course, we spent it within about five minutes of having it . . . but the owners from before, they were losing a million a month." Killen's report continued:

> When Pollard told his former bosses at Canwest of his company's gains, "they laughed at me," he says. "They said 'big deal,' and I said 'well, how much did you make?'"
>
> It is a big deal, he presses. In an age when local television stations are struggling to make ends meet and many broadcasters are carrying millions of dollars in debt, modest profits are nothing to scoff at. If Canwest was losing a million a month the year before the employees took over, this means CHEK's employee-owned operation had essentially made one million and 250 dollars more than Canwest did.

BY THE SUMMER OF 2012, CHEK's new owners had certainly proven Canwest wrong in its July 2009 statement that there were "no viable options for CHEK-TV in Victoria." Optimism was the order of the day—but station insiders agreed it was still too soon to call the CHEK "experiment" an unqualified success.

"We're not out of the woods," said longtime reporter Bruce Kirkpatrick as the station approached its third anniversary as an employee-owned entity. "The common belief in business is that it takes you five years to either make it or break it. Well, we're in Year 3 now . . . We're staying afloat, but we're not there yet."

Financial sustainability remained CHEK's number one challenge. "Our goal is to be profitable, that's it," said president John Pollard at the time. "We are really at a break-even position. But there's always been something else thrown in. Year 1, we had to build two control rooms . . . and that was a big chunk of dough. Year 2, we bought the building. And then we had to upgrade our transmitter . . . That was worth about half a million dollars."

Still, Pollard had faith in the future of the model, as did most others at the station. With these major financial hits behind them, they believed they could finally get on with the business of running the TV station—maybe even start making the profit they craved. They were certainly not prepared for the Year 3 financial punch the CRTC was about to throw at them.

REALITY CHECK (2012–14)

Make no mistake: an employee-ownership model—and the transition
required to implement it—is not for the faint of heart.

—**Tracey Peever,** *Advantage* magazine, 2013

SEVEN WEEKS BEFORE CHEK'S third anniversary as an employee-owned
entity, the CRTC released the results of its April 2012 review of the
LPIF, the Local Programming Improvement Fund. For TV stations in
mid-sized markets, including CHEK, the news was devastating.

The July 18, 2012, announcement read: "Following a public hearing, the CRTC has decided that the LPIF has fulfilled its purpose
and will be phased out by August 31, 2014." That phasing out was to
begin immediately, with stations losing one-third of their LPIF dollars
in the 2012–13 season. That meant CHEK was going to lose about
$700,000—money it had already allocated in its fall budget.

"It's going to be a financial hardship for us, no question," said
CHEK president John Pollard, the day he heard the news of the
LPIF's demise. "Since we opened the place, we've been working
towards not needing the LPIF,—that's been our plan . . . so we'll just
have to accelerate that. Do I think it will be easy? No, I don't think
it will be easy. But this has never been easy from the get-go . . . We'll

survive. We have so far. We've already done the impossible, so we'll just continue to do that."

Like Pollard, news director Rob Germain was jarred by the announcement, but said he didn't believe it would spell the end of CHEK. The station "is still a work in progress," he said at the time. "With the LPIF hitch, clearly it's going to be an ongoing challenge for a long time. But I think we have a potential to live up to here, and I think we can do it."

Pollard and Germain may have retained their optimism about CHEK's future in spite of the LPIF news, but outside their offices that day was an air of despair. Station employees were visibly deflated when they heard they were losing the LPIF. It was a huge jolt to the station's operations and morale—a blow from which CHEK is still smarting.

THE END OF THE LPIF

News of the LPIF's demise was not entirely unexpected. It just hadn't been expected to come so quickly—or with such an unreasonable timeline. Broadcast outlets across the country that had, for months, been planning and committing funds to their 2012–13 programming schedules now found themselves with just a few weeks to make up for the first wave of lost LPIF revenue.

The rationale for eliminating the fund, wrote CRTC secretary general John Traversy in the July 18, 2012, decision document, was that the LPIF had served its purpose, and TV stations no longer needed it:

> It is the Commission's view that the LPIF has successfully contributed to maintaining, and in several cases increasing, local programming, as well as to sustaining the local stations that provide such programming both through and following the economic downturn . . .
>
> While the implementation of the LPIF was appropriate to address the issues facing local stations at the time at

. . . continued on next page

which the LPIF was introduced, the Commission is of the view that reliance on LPIF funding is not sustainable in the long term in the context of the new broadcasting environment . . .

Further, the Commission notes that in the years since the economic downturn, there has been a general rebound in the aggregate advertising revenues of conventional television stations, with a number of LPIF-eligible stations returning to levels similar to those preceding the recession.

CHEK president John Pollard disagreed. Of course, he worried about what this news would mean for CHEK's future. But he said he was even more concerned about what the CRTC's decision to slash the LPIF would mean to small- and medium-market television stations across the country. The sudden lack of the LPIF put independent television stations, including CHEK, in particular peril, he said:

In this time of consolidation, it bodes poorly for independent television. I fully understood that we were doing what we were supposed to do. We've been granted a licence to be a Canadian local television station, and I thought we were living up to that. [The LPIF] was certainly a help. I don't see that the financial markets have changed dramatically enough to say [economic difficulties] are not a big deal any more. It's certainly not a big deal if you're vertically integrated. But if you're not, it's much tougher.

The benefactors of this sudden cut to the LPIF were the cable and satellite providers that financed the fund, most of which were divisions of vertically integrated corporations. These service providers had been contributing 1.5 per cent of their gross revenues to finance the LPIF, contributions that were to decrease immediately to 1 per cent in the 2012–13 broadcast year and to 0.5 per cent the following year.

. . . continued on next page

What this meant for a vertically integrated operation was that one part of the company (the cable or satellite provider) was saving money, while another part of the organization (a mid-market TV station) was losing money. Independent stations like CHEK and CHCH in Hamilton only saw the losing-money side of the equation. For CHEK, the first-year loss was about $700,000. For CHCH, it was in the order of $1.7 million.

To Konrad von Finckenstein, whose five-year term as CRTC chair ended in January 2012, just before the LPIF review began, the decision to end the fund was "very poor." He said a cut in service-providers' contributions to 1 per cent was fair. And the CRTC should have reinstated the original purpose of the LPIF—to support incremental programming, rather than covering day-to-day costs. "But I never thought for a moment it would be abolished," he said.

One of the main criticisms of the program was that the CBC "got the lion's share of the LPIF. A lot of people had a lot of problems with that, saying the CBC is a state-owned enterprise, and if [the CBC's] local stations need money, then let's give more money to the CBC . . . but this is not the way to do it." Von Finckenstein, who had been at the helm when the CRTC established the LPIF, "one of our better initiatives," predicted the loss of the fund for mid-market stations would be "quite devastating."

In its July 2012 decision statement, the CRTC said that any successes enjoyed by mid-market television stations because of the LPIF had "ultimately been achieved primarily at a cost to Canadians who pay the subscriber fees from which the LPIF is derived." The document noted that the commission remained "sensitive . . . to the issues facing small-market and independent stations," such as CHEK and CHCH, and promised that the CRTC "will continue to monitor their situation."

At the April 2012 LPIF hearings, twenty-seven interveners supported cutting the program, while 586 others—including businesses, cultural organizations, elected officials, and government institutions—lobbied for the LPIF to continue. ∎

IN JANUARY 2012, LONGTIME print and broadcast journalist Jim Beatty moved into the anchor chair at CHEK, becoming the face of the station's flagship 5 o'clock newscast. A few months earlier, when then-anchor Scott Fee had announced he was leaving Victoria to take a job with Global Calgary, CHEK management "courted" Beatty for the key position. He was Victoria bureau chief for CTV Vancouver at the time.

Beatty said he was intrigued by "the story of CHEK—the little engine that could story." But his main reason for taking the job was to expand his journalism career. Shifting from reporter to anchor "was just a progression in journalism," he said. "You become a better journalist, I feel, if you do more within this business. You learn so much more."

That's not to say Beatty made the decision to move to CHEK lightly. After all, he had a great gig at CTV. It allowed him to live in Victoria while working for a major Vancouver television station, one that was part of a stable, national network.

"I asked all the questions about financial viability, and I asked the questions about longevity and profitability, . . . and [CHEK management] gave me answers that were reassuring, because I was taking a risk," he said. "I felt the station was a real success. When I was hired, things looked bright."

But within six months of Beatty's move to CHEK, "things took a dramatic turn," when the CRTC announced the end of the LPIF. "The bright future was, in some ways, aided by the LPIF money, and the withdrawal of the LPIF money cast a shadow on this company," he said. "I don't regret making this move at all, but . . . the sunshine that I bought into was immediately clouded over, and it has frankly been that way ever since. The cloud has only gotten darker. We all are very hopeful that the sun will shine again—just to follow that metaphor—but it has been tough times."

In the short term, to offset the first wave of lost LPIF funding, CHEK dropped its late-night weekend newscasts and reduced the number of news updates it produced on weekdays. In addition, the station cancelled a major technical upgrade scheduled for the 2012–13 season.

The plan had been to convert CHEK's newscasts to high definition that year. The transmitter, control room, and master control were ready for the switch. But the loss of LPIF revenue meant CHEK couldn't spare the cash to buy the HD cameras it needed to complete the transition. CHEK has yet to make the switch to HD.

On the upside, the addition of *Wheel of Fortune* and *Jeopardy!* in September 2012 gave salespeople a pair of highly rated products to sell regionally and nationally. Some new Island-produced programs offered extra options for local advertisers as well. And CHEK hired an additional salesperson, Karin Hanwell, that fall.

At first, *Wheel* and *Jeopardy!* brought in "the revenue that was expected," said Bill Pollock in April 2014. But even the cachet of those big-name shows wasn't enough to stave off falling national and regional sales the following year, the 2013–14 broadcast season. "This year, the revenues are down, and that's just the economy. That's everybody right across the country, no matter what the show is. Everybody is feeling the pinch."

Local sales also softened somewhat in 2013, said Pollock. Long-term advertisers continued to buy airtime on the station's highly rated newscasts, but many spent less than in the past. "People are more careful about where they're spending the money and when they're spending the money."

Like all TV stations, CHEK's non-local sales account for a significant portion of its ad revenues. That means CHEK must offer programming its ad agencies in Vancouver and Toronto can sell. "One of the challenges the station has is finding programming that's going to appeal to that national audience," said sales rep Howard Harding. "What is going to continue to interest our national and regional advertisers?"

It's an industry-wide dilemma right now. Television audiences are tuning out, and online and iPad audiences are tuning in to different things—meaning advertisers are turning away from traditional media as venues to sell their wares. But this downturn in ad sales doesn't hit all TV stations equally. Most are part of networks that have collective advertiser appeal, or they are divisions of vertically integrated organizations that have other revenue sources. "If they lose money or if they don't make as much money, they're supported, where CHEK is a single entity," said Harding. "There's no safety net, so that's a bit of a concern."

In January 2013, with the station struggling to make ends meet, all CHEK staff, union and non-union, agreed to take a 5 per cent wage cut. They took a second pay cut, for a total of 6.5 per cent, nine months later. When the first LPIF rollback hit, the station also stopped replacing every employee who quit or retired. Today, the station has sixty-four employees, down from a post-purchase high of seventy-five.

To prepare for the second wave of LPIF cuts, set to hit in the fall of 2013, CHEK's initially hands-off board of directors became more involved in reviewing the station's finances and high-level operations. "We're looking at everything to try to make a go of it," said board chair Levi Sampson. "When business conditions change, when you're hit with something like the clawback of the LPIF, you've got to address it. You have to be proactive rather than the other way around. . . . You have to constantly look at ways to save money, try to beef up your sales, and get more support from the community in general. Those are the three areas we're looking at."

ON MARCH 1, 2013, CHEK experienced the first major organizational upheaval of its independent existence when company president John Pollard left the station. Accountant Rod Munro moved on the same day.

Pollard was temporarily replaced by veteran broadcaster and former CHEK general manager Roy Gardner, who had worked at the Victoria station during the 1970s and '80s. Gardner left CHEK in 1987 to pursue executive roles with BCTV and Global BC in Vancouver. He retired to the Okanagan in 2008, but agreed to come out of retirement when CHEK's board of directors called on him in 2013.

"His years of experience speak for themselves," said Sampson in a March 2013 *Times Colonist* article. "He's got an extensive background in programming and everything else, and he's our man."

Gardner's main tasks at CHEK were to review programming issues and costs—his area of particular expertise—and to oversee the transition to a new executive team.

"He was our interim GM, and he did it for a dollar," said Germain. "We paid his expenses, but he got nothing out of it. He wants to see this station succeed. He wants to see it survive because he worked here for a long time, and he oversaw it when he was in Vancouver. He felt an affinity for this station and he wanted to see it continue."

In May, Gardner handed over the reins of the station to newly appointed general manager Bill Pollock, CHEK's longtime operations and program manager.

"When I got into this business, it was always my dream that eventually I would become the general manager of a television station," said Pollock. "I wish it had been under different circumstances, but . . . I figured, well, I've been doing this for forty years, now's as good a time as any."

At the same time, Peggy Heyer, manager of human resources and accounts payable, became director of finance and human resources, and account manager Karin Hanwell was promoted to sales manager.

Before Gardner left the station on May 31, CHEK cancelled its noon newscast. "The audience isn't there to support it and neither are advertisers. It makes sense to pull back," Gardner told the *Times Colonist*.

Eliminating that newscast meant the station could cut 1.2 full-time equivalents. But nobody was laid off, said Pollock. "We had given some people notice of reduction of hours or layoffs, but it worked out that we just took those people and moved them into other areas."

After filling its lunch-hour time slot with a variety of programming through the summer, CHEK began airing CBC Vancouver's noon newscast in September 2013.

Meanwhile, in the summer of 2013, with one year to go before the final third of its LPIF revenue was to evaporate, a struggling CHEK appealed to the CRTC. Station management proposed that the commission allow CHEK to share in the Small Market Local Programming Fund (SMLPF), even though the Greater Victoria area did not qualify under the fund's population restrictions.

"As an independent, we believe CHEK should qualify for SMLPF," wrote Pollock in the CHEK Media Group's August 2013 submission. "While our market size exceeds the 300,000 population threshold, all other [SMLPF] eligible stations are in single-station markets. Victoria is, of course, in a two-station market with a CMA [central market area] of 340,000," meaning each station could be seen as serving 170,000 people, well under the 300,000 population threshold.

CHEK's application also argued that in recent years, the CRTC had "unintentionally" given a leg-up to CIVI, Victoria's other TV station, and CHEK was paying the price for it. "CHEK cannot compete in the existing market where preferential financial considerations are afforded to our competition—especially when that competitor already enjoys advantages as part of Canada's largest media entity."

The CRTC disagreed, and in its December 2013 response to CHEK's application, stated that the small market fund was not designed "to offset . . . competitive pressures that may be faced by independent operators," meaning the impact of CIVI was "of no relevance in this matter."

Having said that, the commission decided that even though Greater Victoria didn't meet the population requirement as set out in the SMLPF policy, CHEK's needs fit with the spirit of the program. In its decision, the CRTC wrote:

The SMLPF was created to help preserve independent broadcasting voices and to protect their ability to operate in an environment characterized by increased:

- penetration of distant signals obtained through DTH [direct-to-home] subscription;

- industry ownership consolidation of broadcasting services;

- availability of diverse programming on specialty services; and

- migration of viewing from over-the-air stations to other programming sources.

The CRTC approved CHEK's application for SMLPF with the following statement:

The Commission considers that CHEK suffers from the pressures noted above in the same way as other independent television stations that benefit from the SMLPF. While the Commission is not generally disposed to grant exceptions to the criteria set out in its policy, the Commission notes that the size of the Victoria CMA does not greatly exceed the maximum of 300,000 set out in the Commission's criteria.

The Commission is therefore of the view that approval of the application on an exceptional basis would assist in the maintenance, on-going development and production of Canadian programming, including local programming that reflects the community, for an independently owned television station that faces significant challenges.

The CHEK Media Group expects to receive $600,000 to $650,000 from the fund annually, with the exact amount fluctuating from year to year. The SMLPF grant certainly won't replace the revenue CHEK lost with the demise of the Local Programming Improvement Fund, "but everything helps," said Pollock.

The promise of quarterly payments from the CRTC's small-market fund would certainly boost CHEK's bottom line, but it barely boosted morale at the station. By spring 2014, the can-do attitude that had saved the station in the summer of 2009 had largely evaporated. Employees who had once banded together to do everything necessary to keep CHEK on air were now deflated and divided. Frustration, exhaustion, and uncertainty had replaced the optimism and pride of a few years past. After two years of budget cuts, declining ad sales, management comings and goings, programming changes, long hours, and plain hard work, something had to give.

So, in the fall of 2013, when Channel Zero—owner of Hamilton's CHCH—came calling with a proposal to purchase CHEK, some employees were ready to let it go. The promise of a new owner would mean an infusion of cash, relief from the day-to-day struggles, and the chance to become part of a larger organization. After all, CHEK already had a program-sharing relationship with CHCH. And the

SMALL MARKET LOCAL PROGRAMMING FUND (SMLPF)

In 2003, the CRTC created the Small Market Local Programming Fund to help independent, small-market television stations that were being edged out of their own communities by the increasing number of non-local stations available via satellite. "The Commission is of the view that the audiences and the revenues of stations serving markets with populations of fewer than 300,000 people have been particularly affected by the migration from over-the-air to [satellite] viewing," stated the CRTC in 2003.

The idea of the fund was to offset lost advertising revenues and to help small-market stations finance the production of local programming.

In 2003, seventeen independent (non-network) television stations qualified for the fund. In the 2012–13 broadcast year, twenty stations were eligible. CHEK was added to that list in December 2013, and CJON, in St. John's, Newfoundland, was added in February 2014.

Satellite providers contribute 0.4 per cent of their annual gross broadcast revenues to support the fund. In its first year, contributions amounted to $5.9 million. In 2012–13, the most recent year for which numbers are available, contributions—and therefore disbursements—had increased to $10.9 million. The calculation to determine the amount each station receives takes into account each station's local programming expenses and the impact of satellite service on its bottom line. In 2012–13, SMLPF benefits for individual stations ranged from $250,000 to $1.2 million. ■

The Competition

For forty-five years, CHEK enjoyed its status as the only television station on Vancouver Island. But when CHUM launched The New VI, or CIVI, in Victoria in 2001, CHEK suddenly faced competition for viewers and advertising dollars.

At the time, the playing field was more or less level. Canwest Global had just acquired CHEK, and Toronto-based CHUM Ltd. had just been granted the broadcast licence for CIVI. Both stations had the backing of corporate owners, and both were being showered with CRTC-mandated community benefits by those owners.

After the employees bought CHEK in 2009, though, the playing field tipped.

Like many television stations, CIVI has a complicated history, having changed its name and ownership a number of times during its thirteen years on air. In 2005, when CHUM bought the assets of prairie-based Craig Media, the Victoria station was rebranded, along with five others, as "A-Channel." Three years later, after CTVglobemedia bought the A-Channel stations from CHUM, the Victoria outlet became known as "A Vancouver Island." A year later, financial troubles forced reorganization, layoffs, and program cancellations at all stations in the A system, including CIVI.

In 2011, the CRTC agreed to allow Bell Media to take control of CTVglobemedia's broadcast outlets—on the condition that it keep the A-stations on air for the next three broadcast years. In its initial application, "BCE [was] of the view that no tangible benefits [were] required in the circumstances," wrote the CRTC, which disagreed with that assessment, insisting instead that BCE provide $245 million in community benefits. Included within that was $35 million to keep the A-stations up and running "regardless of their financial performance." Without that cash infusion, BCE had acknowledged to the CRTC that "the continued operation of the A-Channels was in doubt."

. . . *continued on next page*

In other words, wrote Etan Vlessing in the *Hollywood Reporter* in 2011, "two years after CTV threatened its loss-making A-Channel network with closure . . . the secondary network is getting a second chance." Deal done, "A Vancouver Island" became "CTV Two Vancouver Island" that fall and was guaranteed to remain on air until the end of the 2013–14 television year.

The CRTC further extended the station's lifespan when in 2013, it approved the merger of media giants Bell Canada (BCE) and Astral Media Inc. In its June 2013 decision document, the CRTC wrote:

> BCE stated that local television stations continue to struggle, particularly in smaller markets, and committed to keep open until 2017 all of its current conventional television stations . . . and to maintain the current levels of local programming for all of these stations. The Commission is of the view that the continued operation of these conventional television stations is critical to providing Canadians with access to a significant amount of locally relevant programming, to the overall benefit of the Canadian broadcasting system. These are important commitments from BCE given the many financial and operational challenges faced by conventional television stations. But for these commitments, the Commission would not have approved the transaction. As a result, the Commission directs BCE to adhere to these commitments.

So, regardless of its financial situation, CIVI will remain on air for at least another three years, with the blessing of the CRTC and the backing of Canada's largest media conglomerate. CHEK, on the other hand, Victoria's independent heritage station, is on its own. ■

Toronto-based Channel Zero came with a more secure, more diversified structure, as owner of specialty stations Silver Screen Classics, Rewind (formerly Movieola), and Fight Now TV, along with three porn channels and a documentary distribution branch.

Channel Zero's interest in CHEK dated back to 2009, when it briefly considered buying all five of the E! stations CanWest was selling.

In the end, the company passed on the Victoria station but remained involved with it via program sharing.

In the fall of 2012, Channel Zero again expressed interest in CHEK, said CEO Cal Millar. "We approached them and asked them if they would be interested in being acquired by us, and there were some people who were in favour of that, and then there were some people who didn't know what to do with the deal." Six months later, Channel Zero again tried to acquire CHEK.

While none of those deals came to fruition, in the fall of 2013, the two organizations found themselves in "discussions" once again, said CHEK general manager Pollock. Because of a confidentiality agreement, though, the board and negotiating team were not permitted to share the content of those discussions with CHEK shareholders—including the employees.

But word of a possible sale got out. "The rumour mill got hold of some of that stuff," said Pollock. "The rumours were killing us. Every time you turned around, there was a new rumour, to the point where people stopped working. All they did was talk about the information they had, right or wrong."

Eventually, after months of uncertainty, those rumours had all but paralyzed CHEK. "Everything kind of stopped," said union president Richard Konwick. "What was the point of doing anything [if] tomorrow everything's going to change?"

In the end, though, nothing changed. The two sides never came to an agreement. There would be no sale. "Negotiations with Channel Zero are over," said board chair Levi Sampson in early April 2014. With pressure mounting to establish a fall programming schedule, and to give salespeople enough lead time to sell ads, CHEK had to move on, he said.

Decision made, management and board members met with all staff on April 9 to address the rampant rumours. "When we had our staff meeting, we let people know we're going ahead as an employee-owned company," said Sampson. In the meeting, he told staff, "All those rumours that you're hearing? Just let those go. We're not under any negotiations currently to sell."

The goal of the meeting was to quell the rumours and to refocus employees who had become distracted and divided. "This is not a game for people," he said. "This is their livelihood, and they support their families and their children on the wages they make here. So although they're passionate about the station, it's also their job, so if ever there's something going on that could affect that, you can understand why people can be a bit on edge.

"The message [we conveyed] was that we're going ahead as an employee-owned model. We're going to continue to run. Everything else is over, and we're moving forward."

Almost immediately, the air cleared at CHEK. Employees finally had information and a well-defined direction. "Uncertainty always causes problems," said Dana Hutchings. "When you don't know where you're going, you get protective of yourself, and you're not part of a team anymore. Now we're saying, 'Let's work together so we can do this.' It's challenging, but we're getting there."

Management immediately buckled down, making decisions about fall programming, holding departmental staff meetings, and planning for the future of CHEK as an employee-owned company.

WHEN SIXTY-FOUR EMPLOYEES HAVE personal and financial stakes in a company, opinions abound about how that company should be run. That was definitely true at CHEK in the spring of 2014. Despite those varying viewpoints, though, everyone could agree on one thing. If the station was to have a future as an employee-owned entity, it needed strong leadership and a solid business plan. And most importantly, those sixty-four employees had to stick together.

"It's time to refocus and get back to doing what we do best," said Rob Germain. "I think if we're all together, and we believe this is the right direction to go, then we can achieve it. We have to prioritize and focus on those things that are going to have the greatest impact, but it's really about us all coming together. We're doomed if we don't."

Of course, the viewing public was never privy to the winter of discontent within CHEK's walls in early 2014. Newscasts still went to air every day. Employees still made community appearances. Sales people still made their calls. Producers still created commercials for clients. Internally, though, it appears to have been a turning point for the company. After the high of buying the station, followed by three years of struggle—and then, just when things were looking up, two more years of even *greater* struggle—CHEK was bound to reach a breaking point.

The good news is that the company was back from the brink, and the employee-owners were once again, cautiously, looking forward to the future. "I feel there's renewed optimism," said Hutchings. "The people who are here are here because they're passionate about this, and they believe in what we're trying to do."

That's not to say CHEK and its employees suddenly found themselves on "this easy, happy, yay-we're-independent road," she said. "We do it because we love it, but it's not been easy. There's no question about that. It's still the David-and-Goliath story, and it's still unfolding."

nine

MODEL TV

At a time when traditional media business models are severely challenged and, in some cases, collapsing, journalists themselves are being called on to play a leadership role in creating financially sustainable journalism organizations. The employees of CHEK-TV have done exactly that, putting their own careers and finances on the line to rescue a local television station and, in doing so, enhance the station's commitment to providing news and information to the community.

—J-Source committee member on why CHEK employees won the first-ever J-Source Integrity Award, 2009

ON SEPTEMBER 4, 2014, the CHEK Media Group celebrated five years at the helm of North America's only employee-owned TV station—a milestone that, without a doubt, warranted popping champagne corks.

Since 2009, CHEK's staff and board members have done the impossible over and over again. First, they took on Canada's once-largest media empire and saved a heritage TV station on the edge of the country from fading to black. Then they created—and continue to preserve—jobs on Vancouver Island in an industry notorious for laying off rather than hiring. They have survived (sometimes barely) every financial curve ball thrown at them, bobbing and weaving their way around obstacle after obstacle. And despite it all,

CHEK News continues to come out on top when it comes to Island viewership and ratings.

That said, this short episode in CHEK's history has not necessarily turned out the way staff and investors envisioned it would when they rallied to save the station in 2009. It is not the Hollywood happily-ever-after success story it was supposed to be.

Keeping CHEK up and running has been described as "a slog," "a struggle," "a tough road," and "a very demanding project." Some characters in this tale have already moved on, others have changed roles, and new players have arrived on the scene. Employees talk about money worries, fatigue, technical challenges, and an uncertain future. All of them would like it to be easier.

Still, each of those employees—along with every single person interviewed for this book—agreed that, no matter what the future holds, this chapter in the CHEK story has been a triumph.

"Well, we're here," said assistant news director Dana Hutchings with a laugh. "No one thought it could be done, and we did it. No one thought we would get a licence, and we did. No one thought we'd last a year, and we did. So we continue to be a success every day."

Board chair Levi Sampson agreed. "It has not been without its struggles, and it hasn't been without its stresses," he said. "But this station was going to fade to black. It was going to be pulled off the airwaves and lost forever, and [after] fifty years' servicing the community, it would have been a huge, huge loss. So, the fact that we're still on the air and we're still providing local news to the community here, that's a huge success."

Former MP Gary Lunn called the CHEK group's achievements "huge, overwhelming," citing the station's importance to Vancouver Islanders as an indicator of that. For the CRTC's Stephen Simpson, it is the owners' innovation that is to be celebrated. "Necessity is the mother of invention, and CHEK has been pretty motivated," he said. "I see they're still on the air, and that's a heck of a long way from where they were."

Whether this short-term success will translate into long-term viability has yet to be seen. Meanwhile, media watchers—in Canada and abroad—are keeping their eyes on this west coast TV station that refused to die. Could the CHEK "experiment" herald a breakthrough for the future of small- and medium-market television in this country? Is the CHEK model a potential prototype?

To answer these questions, it's important to recognize there are, in fact, two models at work here—CHEK's one-of-a-kind ownership structure and its hyper-local programming, or content, configuration.

Ownership Model

The CHEK employee group may have been the first in Canada to successfully buy its own TV station, but it wasn't the only one to try. In the summer of 2009, when Canwest announced it would close Red Deer's CHCA, employees briefly considered buying the fifty-three-year-old outlet. Nothing came of their efforts. "The Red Deer crew [twenty employees at the time] was too small to attempt an employee buyout," reported the *Globe and Mail* in 2009. "Worse, there was no groundswell of support."

On August 31, 2009, CHCA became the first Canadian television station to fade to black in twenty-two years, leaving Alberta's third-largest city without a local television newscast. In the past, outlets slated to go dark had either been revived by new owners or become repeaters for other networks, but that was not the case for the Red Deer station. In December 2009, the CRTC revoked CHCA's licence, the first withdrawal of a television broadcast licence in Canadian history. In Red Deer (population 92,000), some residents may have mourned the passing of CHCA, but others didn't even notice. Because CHCA was not available on satellite, many of the city's residents hadn't been able to watch the station's local newscasts for years.

Coincidentally, a month after the Red Deer station closed its doors, a CBC affiliate in Brandon, Manitoba, became the second-ever Canadian station to go off air. After a number of transactions and takeovers between 2007 and 2009, Brandon's CKX-TV had ended up in the hands of CTV, which in turn tried to sell the station. After two potential purchase deals fell through, CTV gave up on the Brandon outlet, shutting it down on October 2, 2009.

In Hamilton, on the other hand, when Canwest announced it might close CHCH, the community took action. "City councilors got on board; the staff talked about buying the station; the community held a rally. There were speeches. People made signs. They brought their dogs," reported the *Globe and Mail*.

In the end, the CHCH employee group that proposed buying the station was unable to raise enough money to make it work. Instead, Toronto's Channel Zero stepped in and saved it.

In Victoria, CHEK employees received the news of potential closure by Canwest the same day as staff at CHCA and CHCH did. Like the Hamilton employees, the CHEK group rallied to save their workplace. Unlike the CHCH group, the Victoria crew succeeded in buying the station, saving their jobs and local news at the same time.

To understand why the CHEK employees were able to buy their television station, while other employee-purchase proposals failed, it's important to consider the community in which CHEK exists.

"CHEK is British Columbia's oldest private TV station, so it has roots in Victoria and in BC, and it has a kind of storied pedigree like no other TV station in this province," said Royal Roads University communications professor and media observer David Black. Add to that longevity the fact that CHEK is located on an island "that is physically isolated from metropolitan centres," he said. "You've got insulation, culturally speaking, because of the physical location. You've got a strong cultural identity that follows from that, very specific to the South Island." More than that, Island residents relish their distinction from the rest of British Columbia's population, smugly so when it comes to the Lower Mainland and Vancouver.

"That's the real crucial part of it," said Vancouver-based Mark Cameron, who was president of the Media One union (M1) at the time of the CHEK sale. "There's a market [in Victoria] that doesn't want to hear about traffic on [Vancouver's] Lions Gate Bridge, and they don't want everything from a Vancouver perspective. 'Your Island's Own' [CHEK's slogan] is more than just a motto. It's really a way of life over there . . . It's really important."

With that pride of place comes a commitment to Island-owned businesses, something CHEK was poised to become in the summer of 2009. That led to an outpouring of vocal community support when the CHEK employees needed it, said sales rep Howard Harding:

People on the Island are fiercely loyal to Island companies. Provided all things are the same . . . most people gravitate to support an Island business, and we certainly found that. People were hugely pulling for us, and [buying CHEK] was an underdog story. It was a great story.

When television originally started, they were all mom-and-pop stations. As other [media] companies grew, they bought out these smaller stations, so to see it return to that was what older people remembered, and they appreciated it.

Fortunately for CHEK, the population of older people in Victoria is unusually high, and even higher in the mid-Island region the station also serves.[8] In seeking support in its efforts to buy the station, the CHEK Media Group was able to tap into the heightened allegiance that comes with that mature population. "An older demographic may be more loyal," said Black. "There is a degree of brand loyalty you see with people who grew up with appointment television," or scheduled TV viewing—watching specific shows at specific times. "Generation Y, the Millennials, are much less given to appointment television."

This mature audience is also the age group most likely to watch television news *on television*—compared to Millennials, who tend to gather their news online or on mobile devices. The Island's older demographic, then, was a boon to CHEK as it worked to preserve a local newscast.

An equally important and related factor was the financial status of the region. "Victoria is a medium-sized city . . . that is among the more affluent of its type in Canada," noted Black. "You have a far more robust economy because of the demographic profile of the Island. Because of the cost of living here, it tends to attract people with money."

When it came time to raise funds to purchase the station, CHEK was able to tap into that affluence via private investors, longtime Island residents with the financial wherewithal to offer up contributions in the hundreds of thousands of dollars.

In addition, said Black, "because the education levels are conspicuously high [in Victoria] . . . you have discerning, desirable consumers, people that advertisers want to get to." That means that when CHEK management was pitching its business plan to potential backers, it could offer up a financially sound strategy based on revenue from local advertisers, rather than television's more typical nationally and regionally based advertising system.

The Vancouver Island culture, affluence, and demography certainly played roles in garnering community—and financial—support for the CHEK Media Group. Without those elements, the employees would not have managed to leap the hurdles necessary to pull together a deal with Canwest.

CHCH in Hamilton, for example, had the community support, and, arguably, a culture distinct from Toronto's, its nearest metropolitan neighbour, but the CHCH employees' bid lacked the financial backing necessary to buy the station. Red Deer's CHCA may have had longevity on the airwaves on its side, but it lacked the cultural distinction and, for technical reasons, the viewership necessary to drive community support. In Victoria, CHEK pulled all these elements together—but it took more than that to buy the television station.

For one thing, it took a financial boost in the form of the Local Programming Improvement Fund, which was introduced at the exact time CHEK became an independent. That subsidy is now out of the picture, but without those early LPIF dollars, the CHEK group would not have been able to buy the station. Ditto for the interest-free loans the M1 union provided to CHEK employees—money that had only become available a few months before CHEK staff needed it.[9]

Without that M1 cash infusion, many employees would not have been able to come up with enough cash to contribute to the purchase— and without that commitment, investors, most notably Levi Sampson, would not have participated in the project.

"You don't want a company forcing an employee-owned model on a group of people that don't necessarily want to be investors," said Sampson. "If it comes from the workforce, and they're the ones who originally come up with the idea . . . I think that's where you can have some real success."

If the employees at Nanaimo's Harmac Pacific had not successfully purchased their pulp mill in 2008, CHEK management and staff may not have had the confidence to tackle employee ownership a year later.

The Harmac story led CHEK management to Sampson, who led to legal advice that ultimately led to lucrative tax credits.

IN DETERMINING WHETHER CHEK'S employee-ownership model is replicable, one factor that cannot be ignored is human spirit. Even with all the other elements in place, had the CHEK employees —and the politicians, policy makers, and financiers who helped them—not been willing to take risks, this story would have turned out differently.

In the summer of 2009, many of the players pushed boundaries to facilitate the transfer of ownership from Canwest to CHEK. The CRTC fast-tracked its process to help CHEK convince Canwest the purchase was doable, with no liability to the flailing corporation. "Asking bureaucracy to go from first gear to fifth gear is no easy feat— it sort of exemplifies that the CRTC is a fairly lean organization, and we can actually do something quickly when we want to," said Simpson. "People think it was really up to us, and we somehow managed to pull a rabbit out of a hat. We really didn't. We just got focused and made a commitment to work fast . . . All we did was, we opened up an express line, perhaps, but we didn't do anything we wouldn't have done for anyone else if they'd asked."

CHEK management's willingness to ask for help was another important factor in this story. News director Rob Germain and then-general manager John Pollard recognized there was much they didn't know about buying a TV station, so they asked for advice and assistance. "John was smart enough to say 'I need help . . . [but] I promise you nothing in return other than my eternal thanks,'" said Channel Zero CEO Cal Millar. "They were committed and trying really hard . . . so [I said] 'Good luck, god bless, and let us know what we can do.'"

The most surprising—and unsung—source of support for CHEK was Leonard Asper. In the Victoria media at the time of the sale, Asper was portrayed as a villain. In reality, though, Asper's personal actions contributed significantly to the success of the CHEK group's bid. According to Simpson, the Canwest CEO assumed significant personal and professional risk to help the Victoria employees buy their TV station:

> Leonard Asper stuck it all on the line. He was a guy who was watching his own life hanging in the balance, and he stepped up and did something that I think was very courageous. He put CHEK ahead of his own interests, and I don't think he ever really got the commendation he deserved. He was under incredible pressure. Canwest was being criticized from every level possible for biting off more than it could chew under Leonard's guidance as CEO, and yet he did the right thing when it was needed.

Community support, financial support, political support, regulatory support, good timing, good luck, employees willing to take a monetary risk, and a management team that "refused to take no for an answer," in the words of sales rep Howard Harding—without any one of these elements, the purchase of CHEK by its employees would not have happened. "There are a million things that could have derailed it," said Germain.

Given that so many elements must align to make it work, is employee ownership of a television station a replicable model? In theory, yes—but in reality, probably not.

Business and Programming Models

While Canada is unlikely to see another employee group buy a television station—especially without a financial leg-up from the now-extinct LPIF—CHEK's locally focused business and programming models are replicable. In fact, in some ways, CHEK has already replicated a model first put forward by CHCH in Hamilton.

In preparing its bid for employee ownership, CHCH staff created an all-news programming schedule that CHEK drew on when creating its own initial all-news proposal. In addition, because the sale of CHCH to Channel Zero happened first, CHEK management was able to pull from the Hamilton station's asset purchase agreement to facilitate negotiations with Canwest. For five years, until September 2014, the two stations remained connected via program-sharing arrangements that allowed the two independent outlets to divide the costs of importing costly US shows.

One thing Victoria and Hamilton have in common that makes for a workable economic model for local television is proximity to—but distinction from—a major metropolitan centre. While both stations rely heavily on local businesses to advertise on their newscasts and other locally produced programs, they are also able to tap into wider audiences that are more desirable to regional and national advertisers. Victoria, for example, is close enough to Vancouver to draw audiences for its non-local evening programs and movies. "We play into the Lower Mainland, and that does have a benefit to some advertisers," said Harding.

The same thing happens at CHCH, said Millar. "We focus entirely on local during the day, and that's really good for the Hamilton, Oakville, Niagara, Burlington . . . area. In primetime, we switch to more of a mainstream, primetime programming, and that's relevant to the entire extended market," including Toronto.

In addition, at an independent TV outlet like CHEK, the "inherent bureaucracy with how the airtime is handled . . . with a larger company" no longer exists, said Harding. "We are in charge of how to sell the airtime. It is up to us. There isn't a revenue management office to go through to ask permission to sell something for a particular rate. We come up with a rate ourselves. . . . 'Here's a product. What do we think is the market value for this?' That's how we proceed."

With about fifty thousand viewers a night, CHEK's suppertime newscast is by far the station's most-watched locally produced show, and the Island's most-watched newscast. "So we sell our newscasts, and that's been very, very successful for us," Harding said. "I think that's what has made a big difference between us and our competition."

Add CHEK's longevity in a marketplace with an insular culture, and it makes for a particularly strong local advertising potential, something other stations in other cities may not enjoy. "CHEK is more naturally a partner to the businesses it has relationships with in this city because it's a local business too," said David Black. The transactions, then, stem from peer-to-peer associations, creating "a sort of synergy . . . that the other TV stations can't quite offer on the same level."

Despite that synergy, economic realities—and new media platforms—have begun to challenge CHEK's early advertising strategy. It's not that local advertisers are no longer buying commercial airtime. They're just buying less of it. They're also shifting some of their ad dollars into online and social media marketing efforts.

Like most news outlets, CHEK is doing its best to generate income from its online news. The station now sells "pre rolls," fifteen-second commercials that precede every news story that runs on cheknews.ca. But the dollar value that pre rolls generate "is a small amount compared to what we make on airtime," said Harding. "It's a challenge, trying to monetize online [content]."

In fact, it is one of the biggest challenges facing mainstream media outlets today, one with a still-elusive solution. "It's not just at CHEK," said Levi Sampson. "It's taking everybody some time to figure out what the new model looks like in that regard. And it's changing so fast. The landscape of how people consume media is changing at such a breakneck speed that it can be hard to keep up. But if you don't, you're not going to be around that's for sure."

To draw advertisers, a television station, of course, must draw audiences. For CHEK, that means presenting news and programming that's relevant to Vancouver Island viewers. "Corporations that own a lot of the media . . . don't appreciate local," said Germain. "They're only looking for the primetime outlet. Local is what we can deliver that others can't."

The idea of offering a schedule filled with meaningful, locally produced programming is a concept far-removed from the long-held industry belief that big-name, high-priced American programming is what viewers want. In recent years, that way of thinking has been called into question. Leonard Asper, in fact, was one of the first to suggest that, as quoted by Canadian Press in 2008, "the conventional television revenue model continues to be challenging—I would dare say broken."

Asper's definition of "broken" was based on his own crumbling Canwest Global empire, which could no longer maintain the double-digit profit margins a publicly traded corporation needed to earn to satisfy its investors. But just because that part of the television model is broken, it doesn't mean the whole industry is beyond repair. What it does mean is that it's time to find a new model—something CHEK is exploring.

Part of the fix for the "broken" television model requires that TV station owners adjust their profit expectations, wrote Carleton University's Christopher Waddell in *Policy Options* magazine in 2009. "The era of 20 percent and more rates of return is almost certainly over," he said. "Whatever replaces the current mainstream media will have to be satisfied with rates of return closer to those of other businesses in their communities."

In addition, said Waddell, "a model for the future will . . . require a renewed recognition that owning a media outlet carries with it civic and community responsibilities that extend beyond simply maximizing profit."

At this point, CHEK staff and management certainly have no grand profit expectations. Given their financial trials in recent years, the goal right now is simply to stay in the black. At the same time, they have no plans to stray from their community roots. "This is the biggest existential conflict within TV," said producer Richard Konwick. "You have people who see what they do as a service for the community and a calling, and then there are the people who see TV as a licence to print money. This is the fundamental conflict."

Rob Germain agreed. "What we do has meaning. The business side is what we try to do to serve this goal. It's not a means to an end. It's the other way around."

When it first became an employee-owned independent in 2009, CHEK opted out of the "broken" television model, steering clear of high-priced American shows that might—but likely would not—draw moneyed advertisers to the Vancouver Island television market.

For one thing, the station's lean budget didn't allow for such costly program choices. On top of that, the whole premise of CHEK's new model was to focus on less expensive, Island-made shows, giving local advertisers venues to air commercials at reasonable rates. The new employee-owners knew that would mean lower profit margins and audiences that numbered in the tens of thousands, rather than the millions, but it was a realistic model for the Island.

Over the years, a sluggish advertising economy, coupled with the technical revolution that's reshaping mainstream media, has forced CHEK programmers to rethink that direction.

They've added to the schedule a few highly rated US shows with national advertiser appeal—a move that initially helped CHEK's bottom line. But navigating and profiting from the new multi-platform universe is going to take more than a few big-name TV shows. "There's a whole new science around programming," a science nobody has mastered, said Bill Pollock.

Television in North America is no longer the licence to print money it was considered to be in the pre-internet, pre-iPad, pre-smartphone 1980s and '90s. TV stations and networks in the twenty-first century have to find new ways to stay afloat financially.

That's not to say that CHEK's Vancouver Island focus is not a viable model for the future. Quite the contrary. Appealing to the local community is likely to become even more important as broadcasting continues its dramatic evolution.

For Royal Roads University's David Black, it may be the "massive vertical integration" and "bulking up" of the industry that, ironically, is paving the way for more locally focused content. "That conglomerization—that convergence 2.0, if you will—creates some space in the market, and in the hearts and minds of Canadians, for a more singular, intensively local voice," he said. "Other things that are happening in terms of the evolution of media make . . . the cultural case for customization, about people wanting an intensely local experience."

CHEK could become, in effect, a specialty channel—on television and online—that happens to focus on the goings-on of Vancouver Island. "We're going to get more aggressive about trying to create that hub," said Germain in spring 2014. "We're looking at models. We've got some ideas of how we want to do it, and if we don't do it somebody else will."

In other words, CHEK's message won't change, but the medium might.

"Five years ago there was no such thing as an iPad, the smartphone had just been introduced and Netflix delivered movies by mail," wrote Barry Kiefl in the *Huffington Post* in May 2014. "Technology is changing so rapidly, the best laid plan is to not commit past the current year but be nimble, allow creative people to take control and respond to new inventions as they are introduced."

As a small, self-contained unit without a cumbersome bureaucracy or shareholders to answer to, the CHEK group may be better positioned than most broadcasters to capitalize on the changing nature of content delivery.

"The demand for news and video is booming with online consumption, mobile devices, iPads, and everything else," said Germain. "People are consuming it like they never have before—and in all demographics. So if we can respond to that by providing the content, it doesn't matter how people receive it . . . Nobody can consume it all nowadays, but the one thing that we can still deliver, our niche, is local."

An independent television station—be it owned by its employees or another organization—has flexibility its corporate counterparts lack. It has the freedom to choose its own programming, set its own ad rates, make its own business decisions, try out new ideas, and quickly adapt when something isn't working. The downside of all this freedom, as the CHEK Media Group has discovered, is shouldering 100 per cent of the fiscal responsibility. "We're trying to be so lean," said Germain. "You have to spend money to make money. But if you don't have the money to spend, then some of these opportunities are going by the wayside."

As small business owners, CHEK staff and management are hyper-vigilant when it comes to spending. They have become masters of the "reduce-reuse-recycle" mantra, diligent about everything from turning off lights when they leave a room to fixing rather than replacing worn-out cables to adopting a DIY attitude for just about everything. Everyone multitasks. One of the sports reporters even does the gardening on the CHEK grounds.

No matter how many pennies they pinch, though, unexpected financial glitches have continued to plague the station, altering its intended trajectory. Without the financial backing of a media mothercorp, it's a constant, exhausting struggle to survive in what is a wildly expensive business. Money that comes in goes right back out, with nothing left over to move ahead.

But it's not as if the company has been "bleeding" money, Konwick pointed out. "We've never bounced a paycheque. We've never not paid a bill. We've never stiffed a supplier. We've never missed a mortgage payment," he said. "To be a small business is a struggle. To be a small business in a highly technologically changing industry that has a high degree of politicized regulation is a struggle. It's all very much a struggle, but it's a struggle we're succeeding at."

Still, if CHEK is to survive in the long term, it needs to develop a new revenue model, as does the whole broadcasting industry. The Victoria station has gone solo in one of the most unsettled and complicated periods in the history of Canadian media. For almost seventy years, TV stations have filled their coffers with revenue from advertisers who want to reach and sell to the masses. In the new multi-platform reality, that revenue model is fading fast.

Fortunately, CHEK is well positioned to capitalize on something most corporately owned TV outlets don't have access to in the frenzy of technological change swirling around them. It has fifty-eight years of community spirit behind it, a "relationship that is going to be the key to our success," said Levi Sampson. "If we're going to . . . be here long into the future, we've got to rely on our community."

Converting that community support to money in the bank, as the outdated advertising model dies, is CHEK's immediate concern.

"Monetizing the internet [and mobile content] is the nut that nobody's been able to crack yet," said news anchor Jim Beatty. "But if you can continue to promote your brand, that's what it's all about. What is CHEK synonymous with? It's known for news. CHEK is news. CHEK isn't *Survivor* and *CSI: Miami*. CHEK is news. That's the brand. So you transfer the brand that's popular on TV as a trusted voice onto the internet, whether it's Facebook or Twitter or whatever. So monetizing it, hopefully, will come."

THE FUTURE OF CHEK

I think part of the future of television is about TV finding its place, not in its kind of generic network commodity environment, but in enhancing and enriching people's sense of space—whether that's telling local stories, or putting the technologies in people's hands in some way, or bringing the audience and the broadcaster together in some kind of collaborative form, a sort of participatory journalism model.

—**David Black,** Royal Roads University

MOST OF THE PLAYERS in the CHEK story are confident the station will survive in the long term, though not everyone is sure it will live on as an employee-owned entity. As with any business, the bottom line is what will ultimately decide CHEK's fate, and its ownership structure. As it enters its sixth year as an independent enterprise, financial sustainability remains the station's number one challenge. With the media landscape in flux and traditional TV advertising dollars and viewership on the decline, the future is uncertain. CHEK employee-investors have experienced so many unforeseen complications in the past five years that they're understandably gun-shy about what might be around the corner.

When CHEK employees and investors became TV station owners in 2009, media observers across the country looked to them to disprove the corporate media theory that local television outlets were money-losing liabilities. Would the "CHEK experiment" change the future of local television?

Five years in, the experiment has not yet proven conclusive.

Certainly the CHEK group achieved a Canadian first the day it bought the TV station. It has also challenged the established, accepted television model and, so far, made a precarious go of it. In doing so, the employee-investors have clearly proven Canwest wrong in its July 2009 statement "that there are no viable options for CHEK-TV in Victoria."

But they can't breathe easy just yet. Nor is it likely that any other employee group will ever do what CHEK's workers have done, meaning this is realistically a one-of-a-kind enterprise rather than the new model pundits hoped for.

In fact, CHEK's own mission today may be less about presenting Canada with a new model for the television industry and more about keeping the station up and running, balancing the budget, and preserving jobs.

Even the most optimistic among CHEK's ranks recognize the exercise has not gone the way they hoped it would. "It is more challenging than we ever expected," said assistant news director Dana Hutchings. "Nobody's done this before, so there's no model or plan for how it works."

Even Levi Sampson, who called himself "the eternal optimist," talked about challenges, struggles, and stresses. "It hasn't been easy," he agreed.

What has kept the group going is passion for the industry, adaptability, and a collective vision. Except for one brief period early in 2014 when the sense of togetherness flagged, CHEK's employee-investors have been united in their aspirations for the station.

Having made it through those few months of discord, they are now back on track as they move into a new broadcast season. And even during that low period, despite the uncertainty, despite the day-to-day struggles, despite the rapidly changing nature of the broadcast business, not one employee expressed regret about taking the leap and investing in CHEK's future all those years ago.

"Even if this thing shut down tomorrow, which it won't, we've achieved an incredible thing here," said producer Richard Konwick. "It's been five years, and we have paid out over $20 million in wages, and there are twice as many people working here as when we started."

News anchor Jim Beatty acknowledged he took a "gamble" when he left his previous position, "a very good, solid, stable job at a stable company with a healthy paycheque," in favour of CHEK. "But I have no regrets about making that jump," he said. "Life is a ride, and you hope it's going to get you to your destination."

From a strictly practical perspective, creative services director Michael Woloshen said taking a chance on CHEK was "the best investment I've ever made. I've been employed for five years now, so . . . it's the best return-on-investment I've ever had."

On the wall in Rob Germain's office is a framed photograph. The picture, taken on August 31, 2009, shows an electronic billboard outside Victoria's sports arena flashing the *Times Colonist* newspaper's headline of the day: "CHEK-TV could fade to black tonight."

Germain keeps this image in his sightlines to remind himself how far the CHEK Media Group has come since that day. "I'm proud of what we have accomplished here," he said. "I always said if we make it five years, I'll consider it a success, and here we are. We still have challenges, but the opportunity is still there. I always said it would kill me the most if we didn't live up to the opportunity we had, and I still think we can do it . . . If we can make it ten years, that would be great."

For CHEK to reach its tenth anniversary as an independent entity, it needs visionary leadership and a solid business plan. Not every one of the sixty-four employee-owners has to agree the plan is perfect, but they need to have enough trust in the higher-ups that they'll commit to working on it.

CHEK's greatest resource is its people—a creative, passionate group that wants this story to have a happy ending. They are people with "skin in the game," having invested their savings to keep the station alive in the first place. Many invested additional dollars when CHEK needed extra cash. All have invested sweat equity, and they've survived five years' worth of emotional ups and downs.

CHEK's second-greatest resource is the Vancouver Island community. Residents rallied to save the station in 2009, and about fifty thousand of them continue to watch the 5 o'clock newscast every day. Thousands more now connect with CHEK via social media.

In April 2014, the CHEK News Official Page became the number one Victoria business page on Facebook (out of about seven thousand). By the fall, it had about 44,000 "likes," 15,000 more than the number two site on the list.

The most encouraging part of this statistic is that it represents a different demographic than that of the traditional TV viewer—young women comprise the largest share of CHEK's social media audience—meaning CHEK is already successfully using social media to expand its community connection.

But those social media users aren't just watching news stories online. They're participating in the discussion about what is important to the Island community. "It's about engagement," said Hutchings, who runs CHEK's social media accounts. "We want to use Facebook and Twitter to communicate, not only to say, 'Here's our story tonight,' but also to ask 'What's going on where you live? What sort of stories do you want to see?' It's a great tool to communicate differently with people."

Tapping into social media, online audiences, and smartphone-app users is what CHEK and all mainstream media outlets must do if they are to survive in the long haul. And CHEK is off to a good start.

Right now, media technologies—and therefore content-consumption habits—are changing so rapidly that even PVRs, Netflix, iPads, and Facebook may be passé in five years. At the same time, the conventional revenue model for the broadcast industry is fading just as quickly. No longer are advertisers simply buying airtime, as they have done for decades. Now they are divvying up their marketing dollars across a variety of platforms.

In recent years, all across North America, media outlets have been laying off staff, even closing their doors because of declining ad revenues and audiences. So far, CHEK has bucked that trend. But monetizing internet and tablet content remains the puzzle to be solved by all mainstream media organizations. Putting employees' ingenuity to the task is a priority for CHEK as it enters its sixth year.

In 2009, when they bought their TV station, the CHEK employees could not have predicted they were taking the leap at the moment of greatest change in the medium's history. Forget staying ahead of the media revolution. The challenge for CHEK and all conventional broadcasters right now is to not lag too far behind when new technologies come along.

This is where CHEK has another advantage over corporatized networks. It's a small, nimble, creative organization operating without a bureaucracy. The employee-owners can experiment with new ideas, make decisions quickly, and act on them immediately without asking for approval from a head office in a different city.

With its relatively modest financial goals and target audience numbers, CHEK is not looking to save the nation's TV industry. It's looking to stay on air—and online and on mobile devices. Its goal is to preserve jobs, preserve local news, and preserve a TV station that has been serving the Victoria community since the days of rabbit ears and rooftop antennae. CHEK has a building full of creative employee-owners willing to do what it takes to keep the station alive, and it lives in a region full of supporters who continue to tune in.

Ultimately, the "CHEK-experiment" may not fix the broken model of conventional television in this country, but it has shown there are other options to be explored and that it's time to look at the industry through a new lens.

EPILOGUE

Stay tuned. We're not done yet.

—Bill Pollock

JUST BEFORE CHEK CELEBRATED its fifth anniversary as an employee-owned TV station, a change in leadership launched a new chapter in the company's history. On August 1, 2014, the board appointed industry veteran Roy McKenzie as CHEK's new general manager and sales manager.

"I see it as my job here to help grow CHEK from a revenue perspective and an online perspective," said McKenzie, who brings to the station thirty years of experience in radio and television management and sales in BC and Alberta.

He also brings his experience with castanet.net, a successful (money-making) online hub of news and information based in Kelowna, BC. McKenzie was involved in developing the website, which launched in 2000. His goal is for CHEK's website to become a similar—profitable—news and information centre for Greater Victoria and the Island. Rob Germain, who remains news director, has been appointed digital manager and is charged with leading CHEK in this new online direction. "It's going to take a lot of time and energy and dough to get that site going," acknowledged McKenzie, adding that raising dough is one of his strengths.

McKenzie's arrival meant Bill Pollock was able to remove one of the three hats he was wearing at CHEK. While serving as general manager, Pollock also retained his longtime roles as operations manager and program manager, positions he continues to hold today. Former sales manager Karin Hanwell remains a sales account manager at CHEK.

As program manager, Pollock said he believes CHEK's 2014–15 season is the best the station has aired in years, with big-name shows such as *The X Factor UK*, *American Idol*, *The Biggest Loser*, and *Judge Judy*. CHEK also continues to run the highly rated *Wheel of Fortune* and *Jeopardy!*, though it has ended its program-sharing arrangement with Channel Zero in favour of a new deal with a different group of broadcasters. With this new agreement in place, programming costs are down and ad sales are up for CHEK.

"And every show we got was [for] a two-year deal," said Pollock. "So now the pressure is off . . . For these [next] two years, we're breathing a little bit easier."

Despite the "blockbuster" shows in the schedule, Pollock said CHEK remains committed to local programming. *Cookin' on the Coast* and business reality show *The Hard Way* have been renewed, as has the popular sports program *Game On!* A design and lifestyle show called *Trend* premiered in September, and a new interview program is in development.

True to its roots, CHEK continues to focus on local news.

ACKNOWLEDGEMENTS

THIS BOOK BEGAN ALMOST four years ago as a research paper for one of my grad classes at Carleton University. I never expected it to be anything more than that. So I must thank Professor Kirsten Kozolanka for recognizing that the story of CHEK and its employee-owners would be the ideal subject for my Master of Journalism thesis.

Thank you, too, to Professor Christopher Waddell, then-director of Carleton's School of Journalism and Communications, for being so intrigued by the story that he wouldn't let anyone else be my thesis supervisor. Backed by Chris's wisdom, experience, and guidance—along with his sense of humour—the research paper became a thesis.

Professor Dwayne Winseck, an expert in the field of media conglomeration and consolidation, and the internal examiner on my thesis committee, gave me more encouragement than he probably knows. His quiet praise in the minutes before my oral thesis defence gave me a much-needed dose of courage and calm as I headed into one of the most nerve-wracking hours of my life.

More than anyone else at Carleton University, I thank my grad supervisor Professor Susan Harada for her academic and moral support.

To CHEK staff, management, and board members, I thank you for your patience as I interviewed you for hours on end, your honesty in sharing your story, and the trust you placed in me to document this chapter of CHEK's history. I must single out news director Rob Germain, without whose meticulous record keeping I could not have pieced this together.

Similarly, I appreciate the candour of former Canwest CEO Leonard Asper, who saved all his emails from the summer of 2009 and graciously shared them with me. Through those emails, along with a few candid interviews, he gave me Canwest's side of the story.

Thank you to Konrad von Finckenstein, who played many roles in the making of this book. As former CRTC chair, he is part of the CHEK story. He was also the external examiner for my thesis defence at Carleton. I asked him to write the foreword to this book because I so value his perspective in framing the CHEK story in the big-picture Canadian broadcasting context.

On the personal side, thank you to my parents who supported me when life got in the way, when I considered giving up on this project.

Finally, thank you to Rodger Touchie and Lara Kordic at Heritage House Publishing for being patient with me as I pushed deadlines and figured out the ending.

NOTES

1. The simultaneous closures led to three conspiracy charges and four merger and monopoly charges (under the Combines Investigation Act) against Thomson Newspapers and Southam Inc. They were charged with "illegally conspiring to unduly lessen competition and with unlawfully merging and monopolizing the production and sale of major daily English-language newspapers." Neither company was convicted.

2. As quoted by media scholar Allan Bartley in the *Canadian Journal of Communication*, 1988.

3. According to the act, "a 'network' includes any operation where control over all or any part of the programs or program schedules of one or more broadcasting undertakings is delegated to another undertaking or person."

4. The purchase price is most often reported as $1.7 billion.

5. In fact, CHEK wasn't the only television station in Victoria. A Vancouver Island, now known as CTV Two Vancouver Island, also operated in the BC capital at the time.

6. News reports at the time stated that the station had been given a one-day grace period, but Pollard said he knew at this point that CHEK would be on-air until at least the end of the week.

7. The exact purchase price was never disclosed, but it was reported to be more than $5 million.

8. According to BC Stats, about 21 per cent of the south- and mid-Vancouver Island population is aged sixty-five and over, compared to 15 per cent nationally. In some mid-Island areas, the proportion of seniors is even higher—in Nanaimo, for example, the sixty-five-plus population is 25 per cent, and in Parksville, it is almost 40 per cent.

9. In the fall of 2011, M1 forgave its loans to CHEK employees, in exchange for shares in the company.

BIBLIOGRAPHY

Abramson, Bram Dov, and Marc Raboy. "Policy Globalization and the 'Information Society': A View from Canada." *Telecommunications Policy* 23 (1999): 775–91.

Ali, Christopher. "A Broadcast System in Whose Interest? Tracing the Origins of Broadcast Localism in Canadian and Australian Television Policy, 1950–1963." *International Communication Gazette*, March 2012.

Arrais, Pedro. "Parsons Greets CHEK Co-workers." *Times Colonist*, January 21, 2010: A5.

Barney, Darin. *Communication Technology*. Vancouver: UBC Press, 2005.

Barratt, Neil. "A Framework for the Future: CanWest and the New Regulation of Canadian Broadcasting." *Canadian Journal of Media Studies* 3, no. 1 (2008): 106–30.

Barron, Robert. "Nanaimo Mills Continue Difficult Battle." *Nanaimo Daily News*, March 21, 2012: A1.

———. "The Harmac Gamble." *Nanaimo Daily News*, October 3, 2008: A1.

———. "Employee Company Takes Over at Harmac: Workers, Managers and Other Partners Meet Supreme Court Deadline." *Times Colonist*, August 30, 2008: B1.

Bartley, Allan. "The Regulation of Cross-Media Ownership: The Life And Short Times Of PCO 2294." *Canadian Journal of Communication* 13, no. 2 (1988): 45-59.

Beers, David, and Charles Campbell. "Creating Counterweights to Big Media: How to Open Up Canada's News Media in an Era of Corporate Concentration." *The Tyee*. February 2, 2005. thetyee.ca/Mediacheck/2005/02/02/Creating-CounterweightsBigMedia/.

Bellaart, Darrell. "CHEK Staff Not Giving Up: Employee-led Takeover of Station Slated for Closure Is Not Out of the Question, Some Say." *Nanaimo Daily News*, July 30, 2009: A3.

Blidook, Kelly. "Choice and Content: Media Ownership and Democratic Ideals in Canada." *Canadian Political Science Review* 3, no. 2 (2009): 52–69.

Brioux, Bill. "Will Townsfolk Save the House of Frightenstein? Rallies for Local Owners Start as Corporate Debt Threatens CHCH." *Toronto Star*, March 15, 2009: E6.

CBC. "CanWest Timeline: The Empire Izzy Asper Built," 2010. (Accessed April 22, 2012.) cbc.ca/news/business/story/2009/09/24/f-canwest-timeline.html.

Canadian Press. "Canwest to Be Junior Stock after TSX Delisting Friday." *Toronto Star*, November 13, 2009.

———. "CanWest global shares fall 16% to 52-week low." *Toronto Star*, October 5, 2002: E2.

CanWest Global Communications. "Canwest to Rebrand Its Conventional Television Station in Kelowna to Global." News release. July 22, 2009. sec. gov/Archives/edgar/data/1158672/000115867209000038/cgccnewsrelease20090722.htm.

CHEK Media Group. "CHEK Is Truly Your Island's Own—Independent and Employee-Owned!" CHEK News. 2011. Accesssed April 29, 2012. cheknews.ca/index.php?option=com_content&view=article&id=74&Itemid=85.

Collins, Leah. "CHEK It Out, E!; It's All Change at CH, and a Name from the Past Returns." *Times Colonist*, September 7, 2007: D1.

CRTC. *Broadcasting Regulatory Policy CRTC 2012-385: Review of the Local Programming Improvement Fund*. 2012. crtc.gc.ca/eng/archive/2012/2012-385.htm.

———. *Broadcasting Decision CRTC 2009-699: CHEK-TV Victoria and Its Transmitters—Acquisition of Assets*. 2009. crtc.gc.ca/eng/archive/2009/2009-699.htm.

———. *Broadcasting Public Notice CRTC 2008-4: Regulatory Policy—Diversity of Voices*. 2008. crtc.gc.ca/eng/archive/2008/pb2008-4.htm.

———. *Broadcasting Notice of Public Hearing CRTC 2007-5: Diversity of Voices Proceeding*. 2007. crtc.gc.ca/eng/archive/2007/n2007-5.pdf.

———. *Decision CRTC 2001-458: Licence Renewals for the Television Stations Controlled by Global*. 2001. crtc.gc.ca/eng/archive/2001/db2001-458.htm.

———. *Public Notice CRTC 1999-97: Building on Success—A Policy Framework for Canadian Television*. 1999. crtc.gc.ca/eng/archive/1999%5CPB99-97.htm#t2.

———. *Decision CRTC 92-220: Global Communications Limited*. 1992. crtc.gc.ca/eng/archive/1992/DB92-220.htm.

———. *Public Notice CRTC 1992-28: New Flexibility With Regard to Canadian Program Expenditures by Canadian Television Stations*. 1992. crtc.gc.ca/eng/archive/1992/pb92-28.htm.

———. *Public Notice CRTC 1989-109: Elements Assessed by the Commission in Considering Applications for the Transfer of Ownership or Control of Broadcasting Undertakings*. 1989. crtc.gc.ca/eng/archive/1989/PB89-109.htm.

Dakers, Diane. "When the Media Mighty Fall: The Impact of CanWest Global's Demise on Select Media Outlets and the Communities They Serve." Academic paper, Carleton University, Ottawa, Ontario, 2010.

Devlin, Mike. "Cutting-edge Style Comes to Island TV: Hip, Youthful New VI Hits the Airwaves Thursday." *Times Colonist*, September 29, 2001: B5.

Dulmage, Bill. "Television Station History: CKND-TV, Winnipeg." Canadian Communications Foundation, July 2012. broadcasting-history.ca/index3.html.

———. "Television Station History: CKX-TV, Brandon." Canadian Communications Foundation, June 2012. broadcasting-history.ca/index3.html.

Dulmage, Bill, and Gord Landsell. "Television Station History: CFJC-TV, Kamloops." Canadian Communications Foundation, July 2012. broadcasting-history.ca/index3.html.

———. "Television Station History: CHAN-DT (BCTV-Global) Vancouver." Canadian Communications Foundation, July 2012. broadcastinghistory.ca/index3.html.

———. "Television Station History: CHEK-DT, Victoria." Canadian Communications Foundation, July 2012. broadcasting-history.ca/index3.html.

———. "Television Station History: CJDC-TV, Dawson Creek." Canadian Communications Foundation, July 2012. broadcasting-history.ca/index3.html.

———. "Television Station History: CKVU-DT (CITY-TV), Vancouver." Canadian Communications Foundation, July 2012. broadcasting-history.ca/index3.html.

Edge, Marc. "Convergence after the collapse: The 'Catastrophic' Case of Canada." *Media, Culture & Society* 33, no. 8 (2011): 1266–78. doi: 10.1177/0163443711418740.

———. "Why Did I Buy CanWest Stock?" *The Tyee*, October 24, 2008. thetyee.ca/Mediacheck/2008/10/24/CanWest/.

———. "CRTC Ruling No Threat to Big Media." *The Tyee*, January 16, 2008. thetyee.ca/Mediacheck/2008/01/16/CRTCRuling/.

———. *Asper Nation: Canada's Most Dangerous Media Company*. Vancouver: New Star Books, 2007.

———. "The Press We Deserve: A Legacy of Unheeded Warnings." *Textual Studies in Canada*, Fall 2002: 1–11. marcedge.com/EdgePDFile.pdf.

English, Kathy. "Davey Made Media Better." *Toronto Star*, January 22, 2011: IN6.

Ferguson, Jock, and Mary Kate Rowan. "Thomson, Southam Cited: Two Chains Charged in Paper Shutdowns." *Globe and Mail*, May 2, 1981: P1.

Flynn, Andrew. "Leonard Asper Steps Down as Chief of CanWest Media Empire Founded by His Father." Canadian Press, March 4, 2010.

Francis, Diane. *Controlling Interest: Who Owns Canada?* Toronto: Macmillan of Canada, 1986.

Friend, David. "CTV Says Economic Model for TV Is Broken, Shuts Two Ontario Stations." Canadian Press, February 25, 2009.

FP Infomart. "Historical Report: Canwest Global Communications Corp. Corporate History." July 16, 2010. fpinfomart.ca/fphr/hr_search.php?name=canwest&ticker=.

———. "Historical Report: WIC Western International Communications Ltd. Corporate History." March 19, 1999. fpinfomart.ca/fphr/hr_search.php?name=WIC&ticker=.

Germain, Rob. "CHEK Employee-Ownership Timeline." Personal document. Victoria, BC, 2012.

Goodman, Lee-Anne. "CanWest Layoffs Mean Further Erosion in Local News Coverage, Experts Warn." *Canadian Press*, October 5, 2007.

Grant, Peter S. "Reinventing the Cultural Tool Kit: Canadian Content on New Media." Paper presented at the Canadian Film and Television Producers Association's annual Prime Time in Ottawa conference, Ottawa, Ontario, February 22, 2008.

Greenspon, Edward. "Bicker, Bicker (The Three-way Partnership at Global TV Is Acrimonious)." *Report on Business Magazine*, February 19, 1988: P24.

Hansen, Darah, and Cindy E. Harnett. "Parsons Joins CBC, Stays with CHEK." *Times Colonist*, April 13, 2010: A1.

Harmac Pacific. 2011. "Harmac Pacific." harmacpacific.com/index.php.

Hood, Duncan. "Could CanWest Go Bankrupt?" *Maclean's*, December 22, 2008.

Hutchings, Dana. *Reality CHEK: Covering News and Making History*. Documentary aired on CHEK. Victoria, BC: September 2010. cheknews.ca/index. php?option=com_content&view=article&id=74&Itemid=85.

Industry Canada. *Building the Information Society: Moving Canada into the 21st Century*. Ottawa: Ministry of Supply and Services Canada, 1996.

Keller, James. "Employees at CHEK-TV Raise Money to Buy Victoria Station from CanWest." *Canadian Press*, August 12, 2009.

Kesterton, W.H. *A History of Journalism in Canada*. Toronto: McClelland and Stewart, 1967.

Killen, Anna. "CHEKing In." *Langara Journalism Review*, Spring 2011.

Kirby, Jason. "Is There a Future for Canadian TV?" *Maclean's*, October 26, 2009: 46–47.

Kloster, Darron. "Dodd Shifts from CHEK." *Times Colonist*, September 3, 2009: B4.

———. "CHEK Workers Told Offer Not Enough to Save Station." *Times Colonist*, August 29, 2009: A3.

Knox, Jack. "Poorer with One Less Voice." *Times Colonist*, August 29, 2009: A3.

Kohanik, Eric. "Breath of Fresh Airwaves." *The Spectator*, November 5, 2011: B1.

———. "Are We Losing the Community Voice? Local News Coverage Is under Threat as the Economic Crisis Rips through Media Outlets." *The Spectator*, March 21, 2009: WR2.

Kompare, Derek. *Rerun Nation: How Repeats Invented American Television*. New York: Routledge, 2005.

Krashinsky, Susan. "In Hamilton, the Show Goes On." *Globe and Mail*, November 14, 2009: B4.

Lampard, Dr. J. Robert. "Dr. Charles Alexander Allard, 1919–1991." In *Profiles and Perspectives from Alberta's Medical History*, by Dr. J. Robert Lampard, 409–11. Edmonton: Alberta Medical Foundation, 2008.

Landsell, Gord, Bill Dulmage, Ross McCreath, and Pip Wedge. "Television Station History: CHBC-TV, Kelowna." Canadian Communications Foundation, February 2012. broadcasting-history.ca/index3.html.

Maich, Steve. "The Truth about CanWest's Collapse." *Maclean's*, October 14, 2009.

McDowell, Stephen, and Cheryl Cowan Buchwald. "Public Interest Groups and the Canadian Information Highway." *Telecommunications Policy* 21, no. 8 (1997): 709–19.

MacEwan University. "Allard Chair in Business." 2011. Accessed May 6, 2012. itsm. macewan.ca/gmcc/chairinbusiness/History/Index.cfm?MenuOption=2& Line=12.

MediaWorks. "About MediaWorks." Accessed April 18, 2012. mediaworks.co.nz/ Default.aspx?tabid=38.

Newman, Peter C. "The Last Days of a Dynasty." *Maclean's*, April 30, 2009.

Oda, Bev. *Canadian Heritage Response to the Report of the Standing Senate Committee on Transport and Communications: Final Report on the Canadian News Media*. Ottawa: Public Works and Government Services Canada, 2006.

Parry, Malcolm. "The Man Who Landed Tony Parsons for the CBC Looks to Lure Two Other Well-Known Broadcasters." *Vancouver Sun*, June 3, 2010: E3.

Pearson, Matthew. "CHEK Staff Say Fight's Not Over; Canwest Preparing to Shut Down the 53-year-old Station Monday." *Times Colonist*, August 30, 2009: A3.

Perkel, Colin. "Ignore 'Noise' of $1B Writedown, $3.7B Debt, Canwest Boss Urges." Canadian Press, November 14, 2008.

Raboy, Marc. "Canadian Broadcasting, Canadian Nationhood: Two Concepts, Two Solitudes and Great Expectations." *Electronic Journal of Communication* 1, no. 2 (1991).

———. "Two Steps Forward, Three Steps Back: Canadian Broadcasting Policy from Caplan-Sauvageau to Bill C-136." *Canadian Journal of Communication* 14, no. 1 (1989): 70–75.

Reilly, Emma. "Skelly's CH Plan Gains Momentum." *The Spectator*, February 27, 2009: A3.

———. "CHCH Staff Launch Bold Bid." *The Spectator*, February 26, 2009: A15.

Reveler, Norma. "Canwest Shuffles AA Executives with Its Own." *Playback*, January 2008: 22.

Robertson, Grant. "Buried Under $4-Billion." *Globe and Mail*, October 7, 2009: B1.

———. "A Week of Reckoning for Canadian TV." *Globe and Mail*, August 31, 2009: B3.

———. "Two CanWest Stations Sold; CTV Deal Falls Through." *Globe and Mail*, July 1, 2009: B3.

———. "Networks Float Idea of Shutting Smaller Stations." *Globe and Mail*, January 22, 2009: B1.

———. "New Rules to Crimp Broadcast Mergers." *Globe and Mail*, January 16, 2008: B1.

Robertson, Grant, Boyd Erman, and Derek DeCloet. "Asper Considers Taking CanWest Private." *Globe and Mail*, August 2, 2008: B6.

Robertson, Grant, and Susan Krashinsky. "End of Era as Leonard Asper Leaves CanWest over Conflict of Interest." *Report on Business*, March 4, 2010.

Robertson, Grant, Nathan VanderKlippe and Susan Krashinsky. "The Battle over Local TV." *Globe and Mail*, November 14, 2009: B1.

Robertson, Grant, and Andrew Willis. "The Asper Dream Ends, the Sell-Off Begins." *Globe and Mail*, October 7, 2009: A1.

Royal Commission on National Development in the Arts, Letters, and Sciences. *Report: The Royal Commission on National Development in the Arts, Letters & Sciences: 1949-1951*. Ottawa: King's Printer, 1951.

Royal Commission on Newspapers. 1981. Kent Commission Report. Ottawa: Ministry of Supply and Services Canada, 1981. epe.lacbac.gc.ca/100/200/301/pcobcp/commissions-ef/kent1981-eng/kent1981-eng.htm.

Sawyer Park, Jill. "A Tough Act to Follow." *Ryerson Jounalism Review*, June 1991.

Schuettler, Darren. "Takeover Bid Would Create Canadian Television Giant." Reuters. November 13, 1995.

Shelton, Ian. "CHEK-TV Marks Year of Rebirth; Employee-owned Station Could Be Model for Future, Professor Says." *Times Colonist*, September 7, 2010: B1.

Sorensen, Chris. "Credit Crisis Hammering Debt-laden CanWest: May Have to Consider Selling Assets into Unfavourable Market." *Toronto Star*, November 1, 2008: B1.

Special Senate Committee on Mass Media. *The Uncertain Mirror: Report of the Special Senate Committee on Mass Media*. Ottawa: Senate of Canada, 1970.

Standing Committee on Canadian Heritage. *Our Cultural Sovereignty: The Second Century of Canadian Broadcasting*. Ottawa: Department of Canadian Heritage, 2003.

Standing Senate Committee on Transport and Communications. *Final Report on the Canadian News Media: Volume 1*. Ottawa: Senate of Canada, 2006.

———. *Final Report on the Canadian News Media: Volume 2*. Ottawa: Senate of Canada, 2006.

———. *Interim Report on the Canadian News Media*. Ottawa: Senate of Canada, 2004.

Strachan, Alex. "Format Change for CH in Fall; Victoria Station Will Be CHEK Again as Part of E! Network." *Times Colonist*, April 25, 2007: C15.

———. "TV Stations Trade Places: As of Saturday, How You Watch Television in This Province Will Get Much Fuzzier." *Vancouver Sun*, August 30, 2001: B3.

Strauss, Marise. "Broadcast 2009: Bold Moves." *Playback*. December 14, 2009: 21.

Sturgeon, Jamie. "Godfrey Group Buys CanWest; Canada's Largest Newspaper Chain Purchased in $1.1B Deal." *National Post*, May 11, 2010: A1.

Taylor, Paul W. 1993. "Third Service, Third Network: The CanWest Global System." *Canadian Journal of Communication* 18, no. 4 (1993): 469–77.

Theckedath, Dillan, and Terrence J. Thomas. *Media Ownership and Convergence in Canada*. Ottawa: Library of Parliament, 2012.

Vass, Keith. "CHEK Employees Cling to Hope Despite Official Word Station Will Close Monday." *Saanich News*, August 28, 2009: 1.

Vlessing, Etan. "Canada's CHEK-TV Saved from Closure." *Hollywood Reporter*, September 7, 2009.

Waldie, Paul, and Grant Robertson. "Stopping the Press." *Globe and Mail*, February 28, 2009: A10.

Waddell, Chris. 2009. "The Future for the Canadian Media." *Policy Options*, June 2009: 16–20.

Weir, E. Austin. *The Struggle for National Broadcasting in Canada*. Toronto: McClelland and Stewart, 1965.

Wilson, Carla. "Another CHEK Backer Emerges; Investor Helps with Time and Money." *Times Colonist*, September 26, 2009: B1.

————. "One CHEK Backer Steps Forward; Other Investors Remain Private for Time Being." *Times Colonist*, September 12, 2009: B7.

————. "Local Investors, Staff Buy CHEK; Sale Expected to Save 45 Jobs; CRTC Must Approve Deal." *Times Colonist*, September 5, 2009, A1.

————. "More Time for CHEK Deal; Extension Until Friday Granted to Review Proposals in Employees' Bid to Buy Station." *Times Colonist*, September 1, 2009: A1.

————. "Employees Seek to Buy CHEK-TV; Staff to Put Up $500,000 but Rely on Investors for Other 75 Per Cent." *Times Colonist*, August 12, 2009: B1.

————. "CHEK Workers Seek Backers; Discussions Centre around Saving Television Station." *Times Colonist*, August 8, 2009: B7.

————. "CHEK Bows Put Aug. 31; 'No Viable Options' for Victoria Outlet and Its Staff of About 40." *Times Colonist*, July 23, 2009: A1.

————. "19 Employees Cut at CHEK-TV; It's Part of a Five Per Cent Reduction by Canwest Global Communications." *Times Colonist*, November 13, 2008: B1.

Winseck, Dwayne. "Financialization and the 'Crisis of the Media': The Rise and Fall of (Some) Media Conglomerates in Canada." *Canadian Journal of Communication* 35, no. 3 (2010): 365–93.

————. "Netscapes of Power: Convergence, Consolidation and Power in the Canadian Mediascape." *Media Culture & Society* 24, no. 6 (2002): 795–819.

Wutkowski, Karey, and Steve Eder. 2009. "Mixed Fortunes for Canwest Stations." *National Post*, August 29, 2009: FP5.

INDEX

CHRISTINE TRIPP

ABOUT THE AUTHOR

IN HER TWENTY-FOUR-YEAR MEDIA career, Diane Dakers's byline has appeared in most of Canada's major daily newspapers and a number of national and regional magazines and weekly publications. Her voice has been heard on local, national, and provincial radio stations, and she has been a television host, reporter, producer, and writer. Diane holds a Master of Journalism degree from Carleton University in Ottawa. She lives in Victoria, British Columbia.